KNITTING TECHNIQUES

Socks

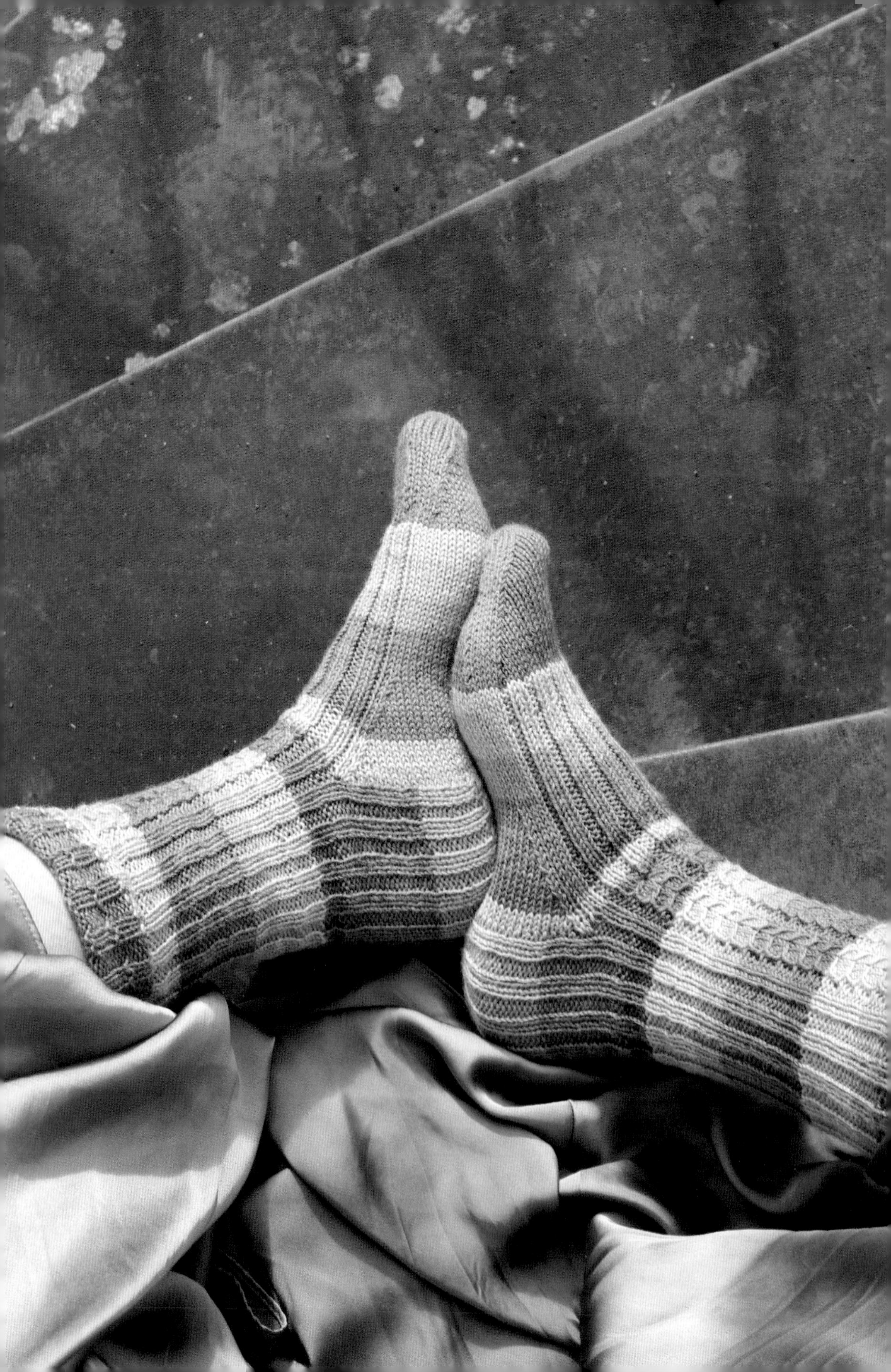

KNITTING TECHNIQUES

Socks

Rita Taylor

THE CROWOOD PRESS

First published in 2022 by
The Crowood Press Ltd
Ramsbury, Marlborough
Wiltshire SN8 2HR

enquiries@crowood.com
www.crowood.com

British Library Cataloguing-in-Publication Data
A catalogue record for this book is available from the British Library.

ISBN 978 0 71984 062 3

Cover design: Blue Sunflower Creative

Photographs: all photographs are by the author, with the exception of those on pages 2, 10, 18, 34, 38 (top photo), 40, 50–55, 57 (bottom two photos), 58–61, 62 (left and right photos), 63, 65 (top two photos), 66–71, 73 (bottom photo), 74 and 76, which are © The Crowood Press

Typeset by Simon and Sons
Printed and bound in India by Replika Press Pvt. Ltd.

Contents

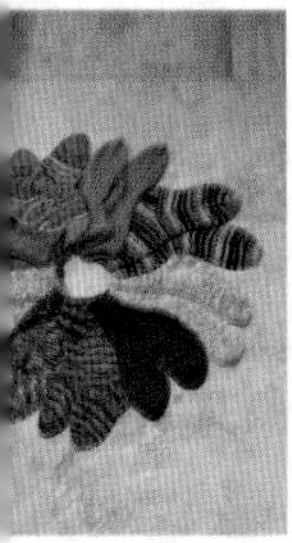
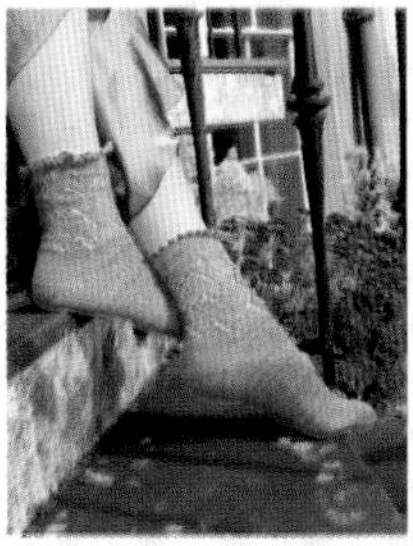
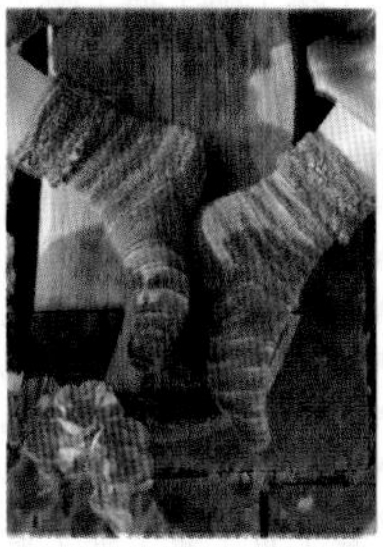
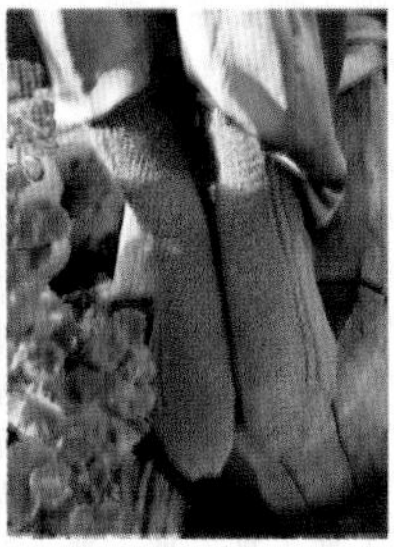
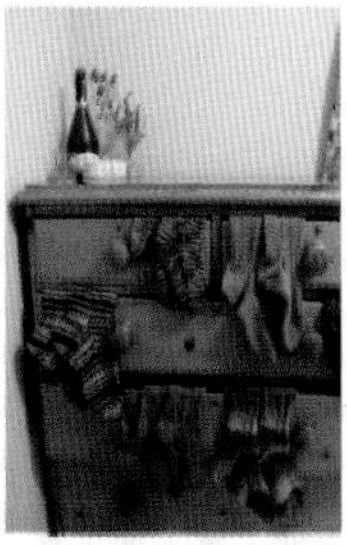
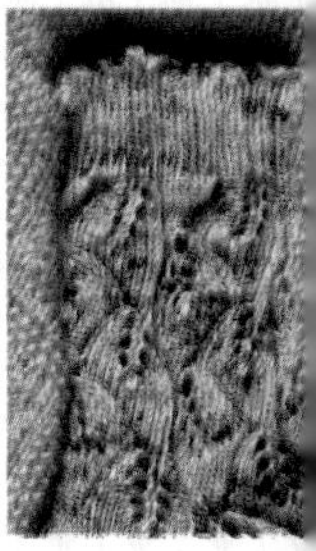

Acknowledgements

My thanks go to Hilary Clunes for helping me to knit some of the pairs of socks that feature here and for her valuable comments on some of the projects. Thanks to Mary Hawkins for sharing her knowledge of sock heels and thank you to the members of North Norfolk Knitters, Pauline, Trenna, Lesley, Jenn, Co, Jackie and Geraldine, who patiently did the hand modelling for some of the techniques, and to the members of my family, Liho, David and Harvey, who modelled some of the socks for the photographs.

Special thanks to my husband who has had to put up with the constant clutter of yarn, needles, piles of notes and chatter about socks. And thank you to the people at Crowood who are always so encouraging and helpful when answering my queries.

Abbreviations and Chart Key

alt	alternate/alternating
approx.	approximately
beg	beginning
dec	decrease
inc	increase
k	knit
k2tog	knit 2 together
k2togtbl	knit two together through back loops
m1L	make 1 stitch in the left leg of the stitch below
m1R	make 1 stitch in the right leg of the stitch below
p	purl
pm	place marker
RS	right side
rem	remain(ing)
rep	repeat
rnd(s)	round(s)
sk2p	slip 1, knit 2 together and pass slipped stitch over them
sl1	slip one stitch
ssk	slip each of the next 2 stitches, independently, return them to the left needle and knit them together through back loops
tbl	through back loop
tog	together
WS	wrong side
1/1 RC	slip next stitch to cable needle and place at back of work, k1, then k1 from cable needle
1/2 LC	slip next stitch to cable needle and place at front of work, k2, then k1 from cable needle

1/2 RC	slip next 2 stitches to cable needle and place at back of work, k1, then k2 from cable needle
2/2 LC	slip next 2 stitches to cable needle and place at front of work, k2, then k2 from cable needle
2/2 RC	slip next 2 stitches to cable needle and place at back of work, k2, then k2 from cable needle
2/2 LPC	slip next 2 stitches to cable needle and place at front of work, p2, then k2 from cable needle
2/2 RPC	slip next 2 stitches to cable needle and place at back of work, k2, then p2 from cable needle

CHART KEY

Key

- knit
- • purl
- O yo
- \ ssk
- / k2tog
- ⸝̇ p2tog
- Λ sl1, k2tog, psso

Introduction

STEPPING INTO SOCKS

If you've never knitted a sock before but always wanted to try, you will find here all the information you need to help you create that well-fitting sock. What might at first seem like a complex piece of knitting is actually simpler than you might think. A sock is just a tube of knitting, closed at one end and with a right-angled bend somewhere near the middle to create the foot. There are numerous ways to finish the closed end that pockets the toe and a number of ways to create the right-angled bend for the heel. Some of them might feel more comfortable on your foot than others. The patterns included here will describe these ways of customizing the basic shape to create a variety of different socks.

A BIT OF HISTORY

There has always been a need for something to keep the feet warm and the earliest piece of knitting so far discovered is a pair of blue and white cotton socks, found in Egypt and dating from around the eleventh century. The flexibility of knitting makes it ideal to create the complex shape that is a sock or stocking. Cloth cut on the bias was used to create the long stockings worn in Europe but, as the technique of knitting was spread around the globe, so it became obvious that the shape of the leg and foot could be more easily accommodated by the more elastic knitted fabric. Over-the-knee stockings, often made from silk and known as hose, were worn by men to go with their doublet or, later, with their breeches. Women's stockings were long and usually in a patterned lace but by the nineteenth century they were ankle length and usually plain black. Styles changed at the beginning of the twentieth century and men's stockings were often patterned, especially those that were to be worn for various sporting activities. Sometimes just the cuffs were patterned and the legs were ribbed; other styles had an all-over pattern of diamonds, known as Argyle. With the invention of Nylon, women took to wearing machine-made stockings in various shades of light brown. But with the trend in fashion towards wearing jeans or plain trousers, patterned socks became *de rigueur* and now there are thousands of patterns available in as many styles as you can imagine.

This book

The main part of the book will show you how to perform a variety of techniques and methods of construction for heels and toes that will create a pleasing and perfect fitting sock. You will also find thirteen patterns here using some of the different techniques to illustrate the various methods of construction.

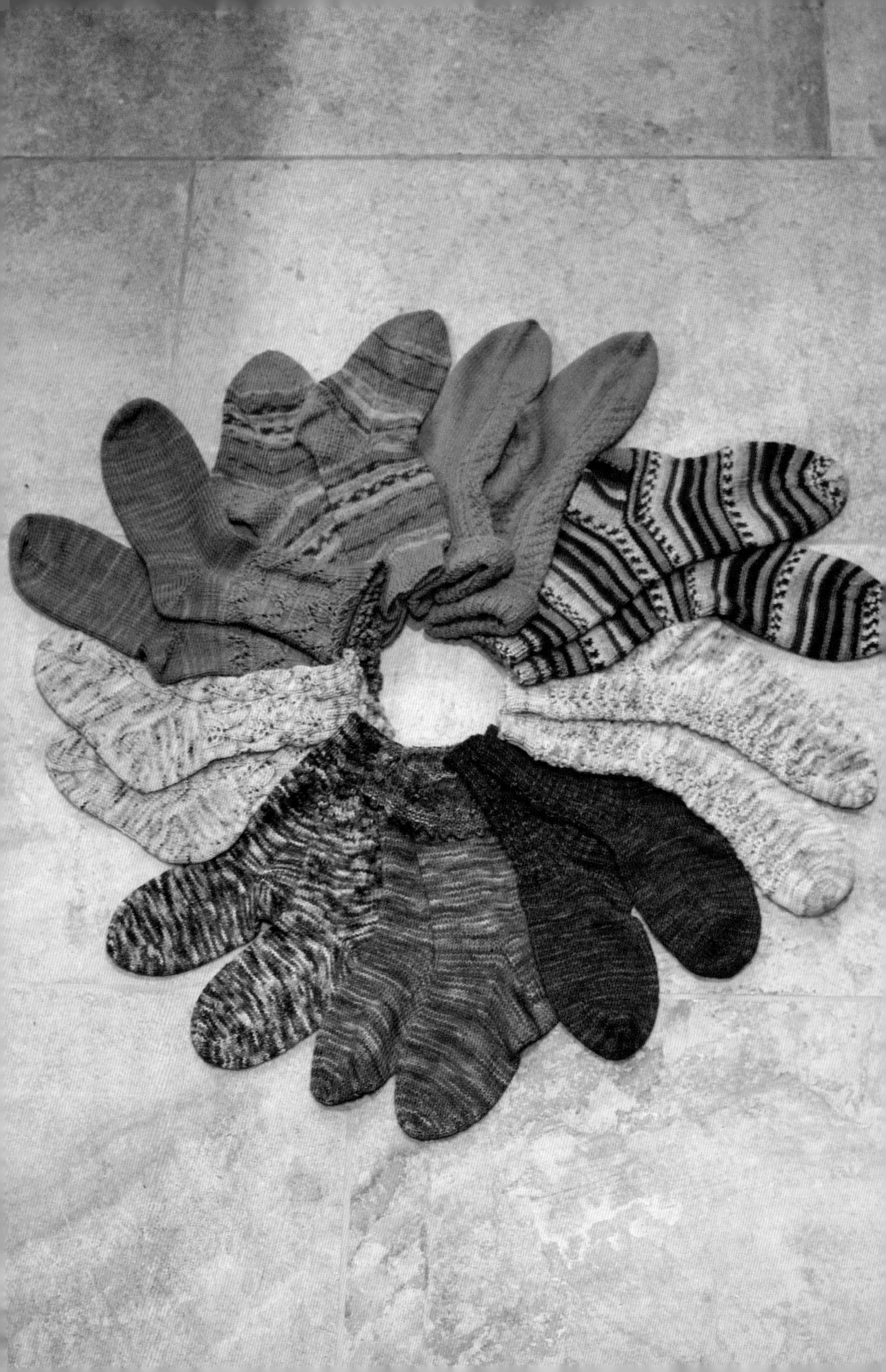

CHAPTER 1

Materials and Measurements

MATERIALS

Socks are very portable projects. The quantity of materials required doesn't take up much room and will fit easily into a small project bag. The essential items are about 100g of suitable 4-ply yarn, appropriate needles, either double pointed or circular, and a tape measure.

TIP

If you plan to do a lot of sock knitting, then buy the best tools and yarn that you can afford. Socks made from synthetic materials won't be as warm and comfortable as those made from natural fibres, nor will they be as durable.

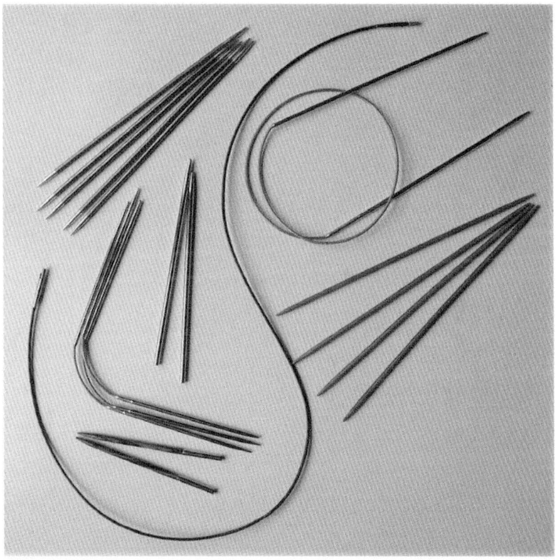

Different types of needles for circular knitting: interchangeable, double-pointed, trio and fixed circular.

EQUIPMENT

The most important pieces of equipment are yarn and needles but, while some additional items are not essential, there are some that will be useful.

Needles

Double-pointed needles (DPNs) come in sets of four or five (occasionally six). It is a matter of personal preference how many you decide to use, bearing in mind that the fewer the needles the greater the stretch between them, which can sometimes cause ladders at the changeover point. The needles can be of different lengths and made from various materials, such as:

- smooth metal, often with sharp points, useful for lace work
- wood, which can be plain or coloured, and is lightweight and warm to the touch
- bamboo, the lightest in weight and also warm and slightly flexible, useful for cables
- plastic, which comes in a range of colours and is also light and flexible but can get sticky, making it difficult to slide the stitches along

- carbon, lightweight, smooth and warm to the touch with tapered brass tips that work easily with the yarn.

Not all needles are round in shape: there are also square ones, and some people find these easier to use. The points of needles vary from the sharp-tipped, often called lace needles, to more rounded and blunt versions. The different materials can affect the gauge of the knitting, so stick to the same type throughout the project. Bamboo and wood needles are useful for slippery yarns as they will grip the yarn more tightly making the stitches less likely to fall off.

Circular needles

These can be fixed, with the cable section permanently attached to the tip, or interchangeable, where the tips screw or click into a length of flexible cable. Different brands of needle often have different lengths of tips but 4- or 5-inch needles are the most manageable for sock knitting. The cable section of circular needles also comes in different lengths and it is best to choose the length that is slightly shorter than the circumference of the sock. A short circular needle can sometimes be uncomfortable and awkward to manoeuvre on a small sock, which is why some people prefer to use a set of double-pointed needles, especially when knitting children's socks. However, it is worth trying different types and lengths of circular needles yourself, if possible, to see which feel the most comfortable to work with in the hands. The needles with long tips can be awkward when knitting socks with anything less than forty stitches.

Some people prefer to use two circular needles, with the instep stitches kept on one needle and the foot stitches on the other but working the complete rounds over both needles.

Interchangeable needles

These needles come in two parts: the tips and the cable of varying lengths. The tips attach to their cables by different methods and some stay more firmly attached than others. Again, they are made from the same materials as double-pointed needles. Cable length varies from 20cm to more than 100cm, although for socks it is unlikely that you would need more than 80cm. These latter would seem much too long for knitting socks but the longer lengths are suitable for the 'magic loop' method of working. Again, the different brands have different lengths of needle tips; some brands have a choice of two.

Trio needles

These are a recent innovation that can be useful for working items with a small diameter. As the name suggests, they come in a set of three and are double pointed (some with a sharp tip at one end and a more rounded one at the other). In between the tips is a short length of flexible cable. They have the advantage over double-pointed needles in that there are only two needles holding

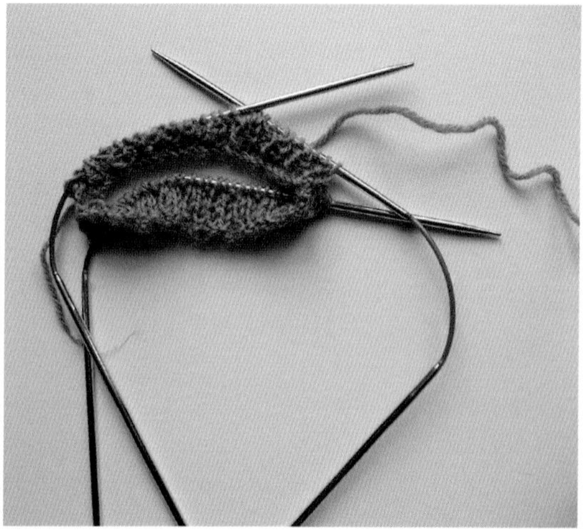
Working in the round on the set of trio needles.

MAGIC LOOP

Working this method requires a long circular needle, at least 80cm, where half of the stitches are held on different sections of the cable. The cable is pulled out between the two halves to form a loop on the left. The stitches from the front half are pushed forwards onto the tip of the needle at the left while the other tip, holding the stitches at the back, is used to knit them. These stitches are moved onto the cable, another loop is pulled out, and the second group of stitches is then knitted.

the stitches while the third needle does the knitting. This helps to avoid the ladders that can sometimes appear when using four needles and also avoids that annoying tendency for the needle not in use to slip out of some of the stitches.

Straight needles

Socks can also be knitted flat or sideways on straight needles. The construction is quite different, and the socks will require seaming when the knitting is finished. After casting on the required number of stitches and knitting the cuff and leg, the stitches are divided in half with the first quarter placed on a holder and the next half knitted for the top of the foot. The remaining stitches are placed on another holder. When the foot is the required length, the toe is shaped in two halves by decreasing at the beginning and end of every alternate row until these stitches are also reduced by half (or more if you have long toes). Next, increase at the beginning and end of each row until you are back to the original number of stitches for the foot. Work the bottom half of the foot to the same length as the top half then shape the heel as for the toe. When the shaping is finished, graft the heel stitches to the two quarters that were left after the leg was finished. Sew the seams at the back of the leg and along the sides of the foot.

Socks knitted in an Argyle pattern are often knitted flat because the required colours would not be in the correct position for circular knitting.

Yarn

The best yarn for socks depends on their intended purpose. Yarn for walking socks will be different to that for socks to wear around the house or for bedsocks. For the type of socks you will wear every day inside shoes, the best yarn is that which is spun specifically for socks. The wool is frequently a combination of Merino or Blue Faced Leicester, perhaps with a bit of added silk for softness. Sock yarn should be durable, usually combining wool for its elasticity and nylon for added strength and its multiple plies are often tightly twisted. The tight twist makes the yarn more resistant to pilling. A typical mix of sock wool is 80 per cent wool and 20 per cent nylon, with the high proportion of wool helping to retain the elasticity that is needed for the socks to fit snugly around the foot and leg. Wool is also a breathable fibre and it wicks away moisture, making the feet less likely to sweat. Cotton or bamboo reinforced with nylon is also suitable, especially for those who are sensitive to wool, but the fabric won't spring back into shape in the same way that wool does. Wool on its own, as

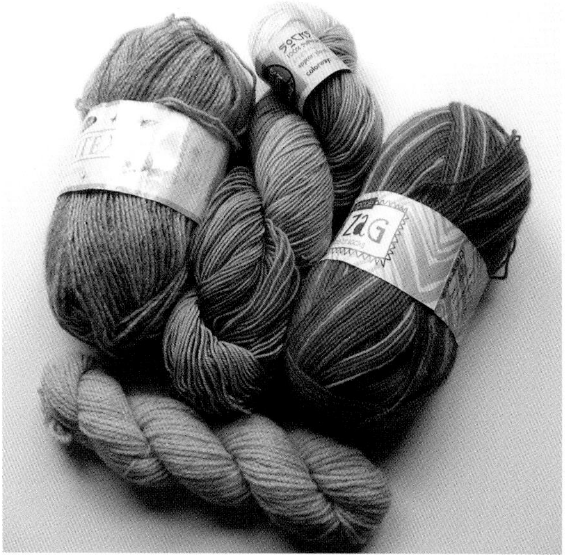

A selection of yarns suitable for knitting socks.

long as it has a high twist, will be more durable than that which is soft and lightly spun. Merino wool or cashmere, while they are lovely and soft, are prone to wearing into holes very quickly. It is possible to buy small spools or cards of reinforcement yarn that can be knitted together with one of the softer yarns at the heels and toes. But the yarn you choose does depend on the function of the socks. Bedsocks, for example, can be made with a soft alpaca, angora or even cashmere for an extra luxurious feel.

Commercially produced yarns will have a ball band suggesting the size of needles and the gauge you are likely to get with them. In most cases, unless it is specifically labelled for socks, this gauge will be too loose. Socks need to grip the feet or they will gather up around the ankles and sometimes slide down into the shoes. Using smaller needles than suggested will naturally use more yarn. A pair of medium-sized socks in a basic pattern will use approximately 400 metres/425 yards so do check the ball band for length and buy an extra ball if you think you may run out.

TIP

If the yarn doesn't have a ball band indicating its weight and the recommended needle size, then wrap the yarn around a pencil. Push the strands up close to each other so that there are no gaps. Place the pencil against the side of a ruler and count how many wraps it takes to cover 1 inch. A typical 4-ply sock yarn would be 18WPI (wraps per inch).

Yarns produced specifically as sock yarn will be mainly 4-ply weight, to be knitted on needles sized from 2.25mm to 3.00mm. Most of the yarns used for the patterns in this book are those designed especially for socks. They contain a percentage of nylon, which makes them more hardwearing, and a high percentage of wool for the warmth and comfort this fibre gives. As socks are likely to be washed fairly frequently, many of them will be machine washable, but if they are not, washing them in lukewarm water and drying them outside will allow them to retain their elasticity.

For walking socks, sometimes known as boot socks, a heavier weight yarn will be preferable, such as a DK or even an Aran weight. These need to be especially hardwearing but also soft so that they don't rub and cause painful blisters. Again, a combination of wool and nylon is best but with perhaps a slightly higher proportion of nylon than that for everyday socks.

Choosing colours

Colour can obviously influence yarn choice. Plain stocking stitch socks look especially good in a variegated or self-striping yarn but if you are knitting socks with a lace pattern then a lighter, self-coloured yarn will show off the pattern better than a variegated or dark-coloured yarn, although a self-striping yarn can enhance certain lace patterns (Old Shale being the best example). Plain self-coloured yarns are best for cabled socks, or a tweedy yarn could work well for these.

Yarn Substitution

If you want to use a different yarn to that stated in the pattern, try to use one that is as comparable as possible to the one stated. Most socks are knitted in light- or medium-weight yarn, which

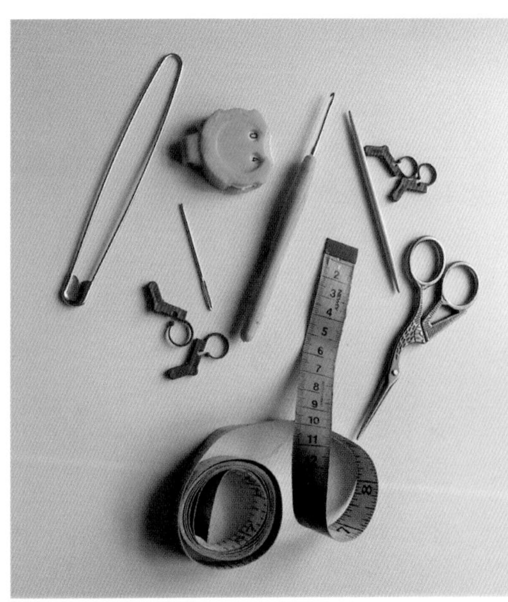

A selection of items useful for sock knitting, including sock-shaped stitch markers.

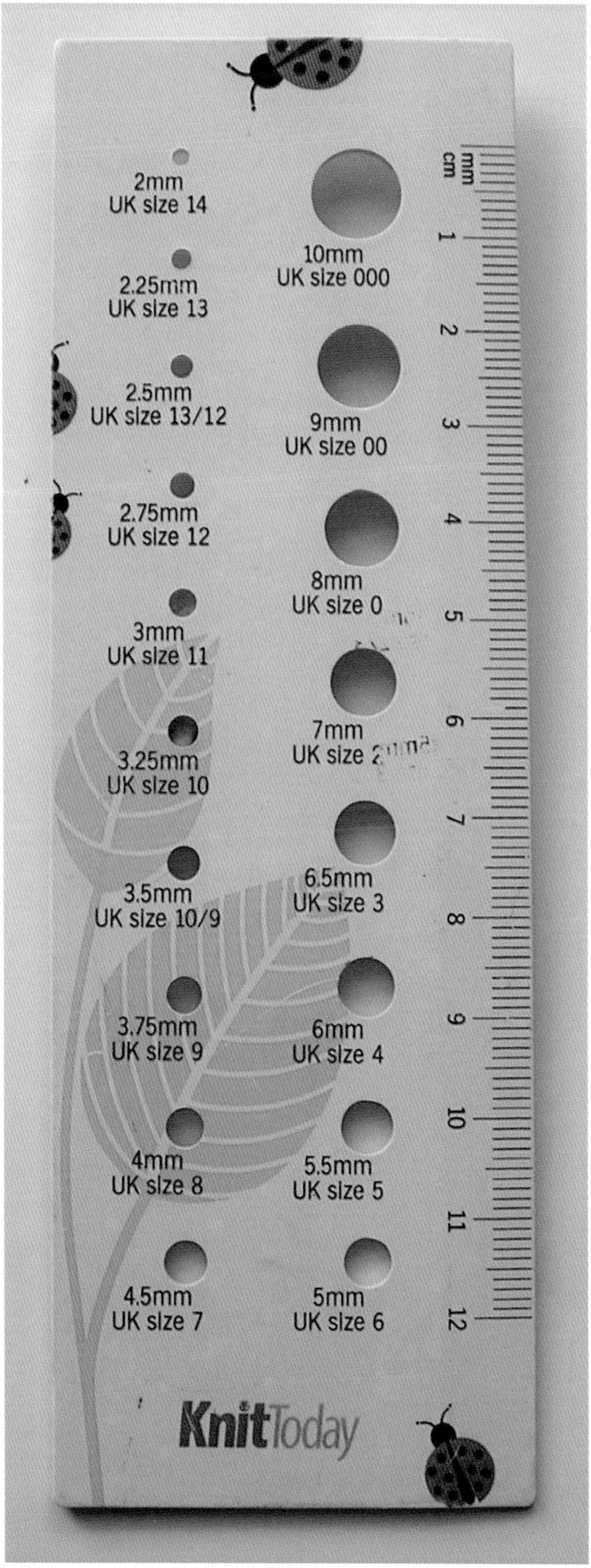

Needle gauge. This one is also marked with inches and centimetres for checking tension.

gives a tension of between 20 and 28 stitches to 10cm (4in). This is quite a wide variation so it is important to do a test swatch in your chosen yarn before beginning. Also note that the substitute yarn might have a different number of metres per ball than the original yarn, so you might need to buy more than that used in the pattern. Calculate the number of metres in the original yarn and then work out if you will need more or fewer balls of the substitute yarn by checking the length on its ball band. If you are following an old pattern, where the amount of yarn was given in ounces, there are 1.75 ounces in 50 grams.

Other useful items

Most experienced knitters will have all the appropriate accessories already, but if you are new to knitting then you will probably want a needle gauge. Not all double-pointed or circular needles have their sizes marked on them. The one pictured also has a measure for checking the tension, or gauge, of your swatch.

Cable needles, straight or U-shaped, are useful for holding stitches temporarily while crossing them. If you are working a sock with a cable or lace pattern then a row counter can be useful, as could a set of stitch markers. A stitch holder or large safety pin is handy for holding the instep stitches while the heel is worked. A tapestry or sewing up needle is needed for grafting the toe stitches together or for seaming a sock worked on two needles. A medium-sized crochet hook is useful for picking up dropped stitches.

Other useful items include scissors or a thread cutter and a pair of point protectors to slip over the ends of the needles before putting the work away. Alternatively, you might prefer a tube that the knitting on its needles can slip into safely. A project bag to keep your work and your pattern together completes the equipment. Sock knitting is a very portable craft and ideal to carry around when travelling; keeping it all together in a small bag means you can quickly pick up everything at once and know that you won't have one double-pointed needle missing!

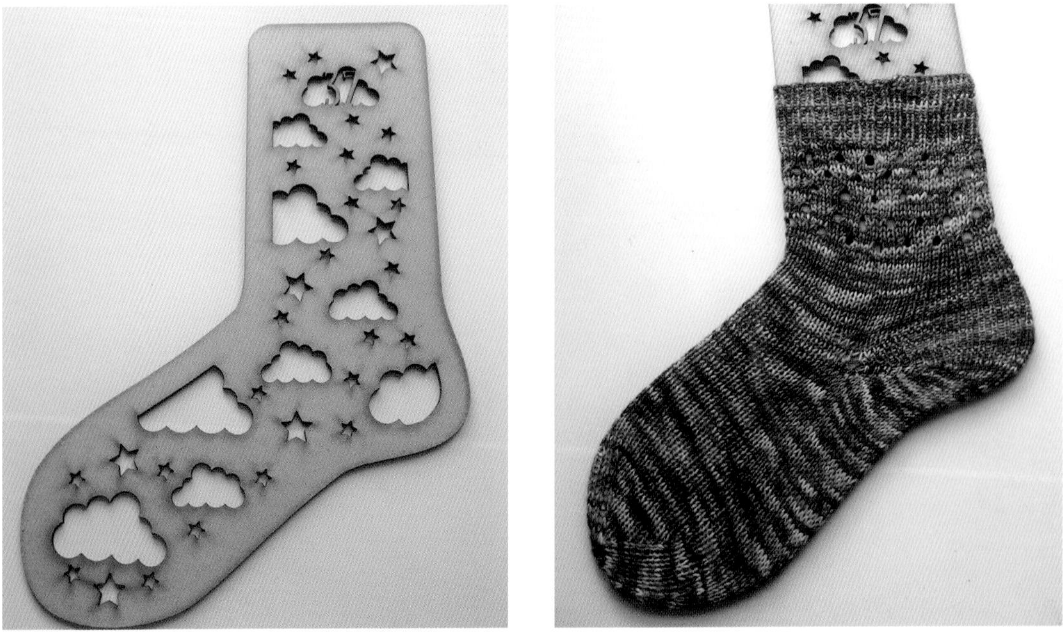

Wooden sock blocker for a size 37 foot, also with the Phoenix sock.

If you plan to knit a lot of socks, then it is worth having a set of sock blockers. These are made in various sizes and will shape your socks so that the heel and toe are in the correct positions and the stitches are smoothed out.

BLOCKING

As well as shaping the socks, blocking evens out the stitches, opens up the lace and makes cables stand out.

Wash the finished socks in warm water either with a little specialist wool wash such as Eucalan or with a drop of shampoo. Let them soak for about fifteen minutes then squeeze them gently to remove most of the water. Place them on the sock blockers and leave them to dry in a warm place where the air can circulate around them. It sometimes takes a day or two to dry them out thoroughly.

If you don't have sock blockers, place the socks on a towel, patting them gently into shape; then leave them to dry.

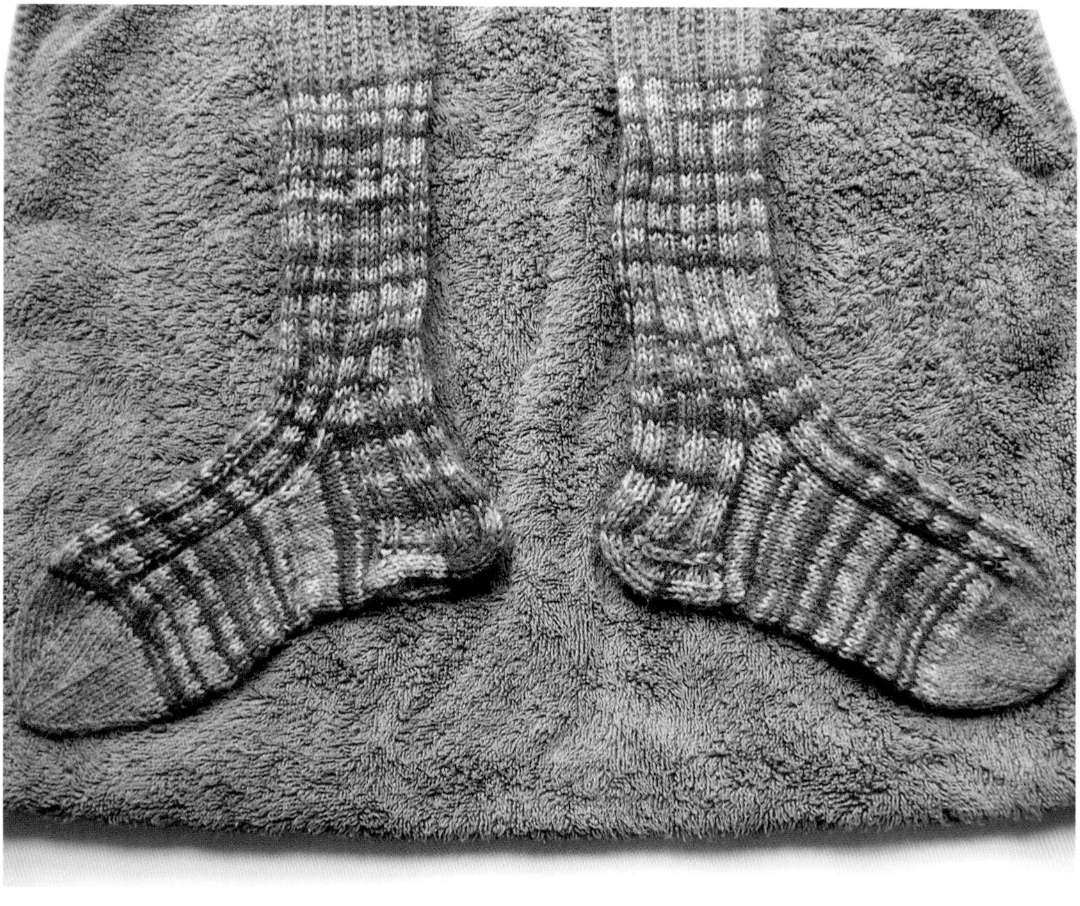

Socks left to dry naturally on a damp towel.

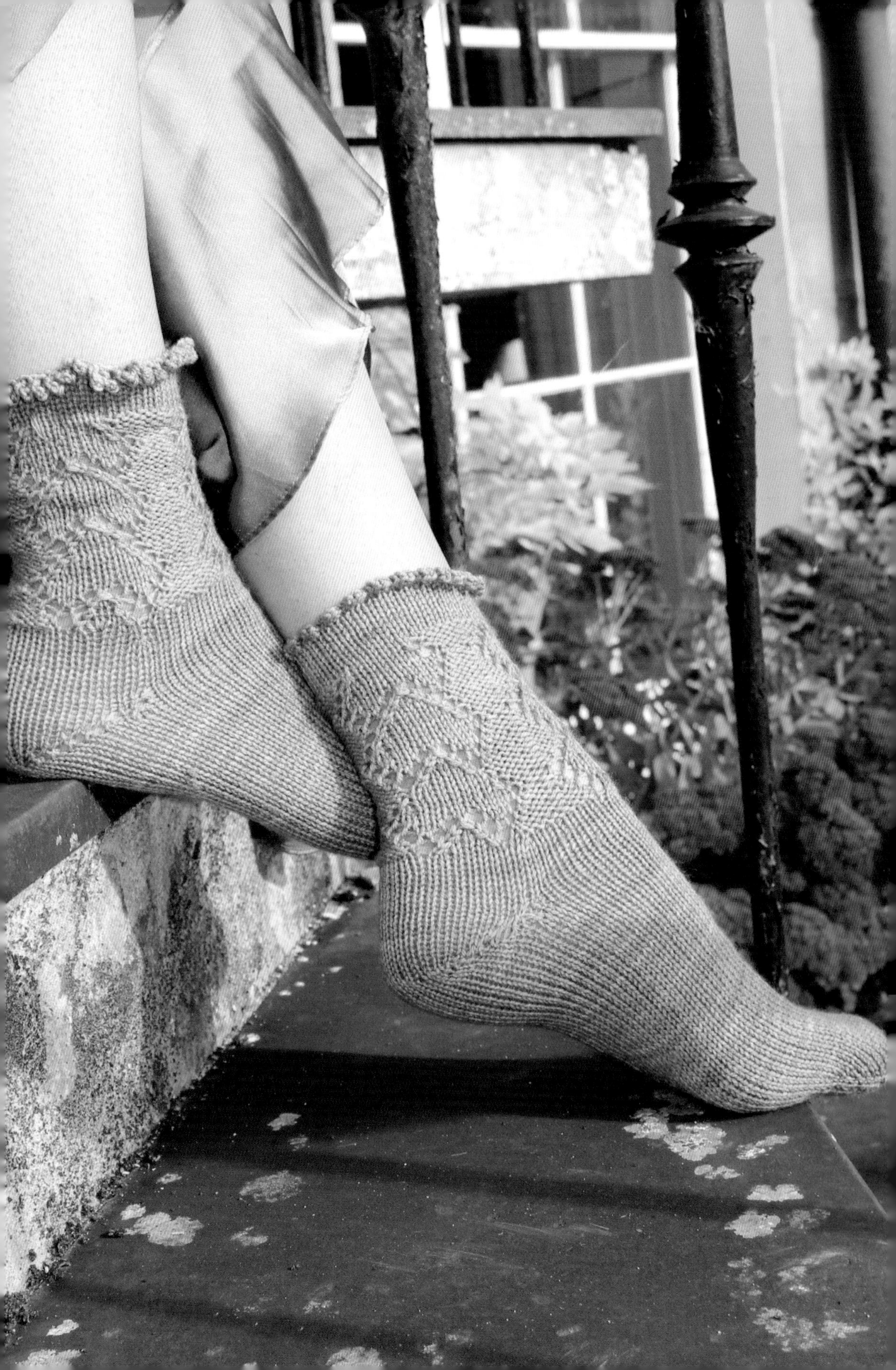

CHAPTER 2

Techniques

THE ANATOMY OF A SOCK

A sock consists of seven parts: cuff, leg, heel, gusset, foot (instep and sole) and toe. If the sock is knitted with a short row heel there is no gusset but the other parts are the same.

Measurements

Whichever method you choose to construct a sock, to get the best fit you will need to take a number of measurements of the recipient's leg and foot. An average person has an ankle measurement the same as the circumference of the foot. A typical heel will require half of the number of stitches that were cast on for the sock. However, some people have wide or long heels and this necessitates working a few extra stitches or rows at that point. Sixty per cent of the leg stitches should accommodate a wide heel. Conversely, work forty per cent of the leg stitches for those with a narrow heel.

The number of rows to work is usually an amount adequate enough to make the heel flap square in shape. For those with a high instep it will be necessary to work a few extra rows and pick up more stitches before shaping the gusset.

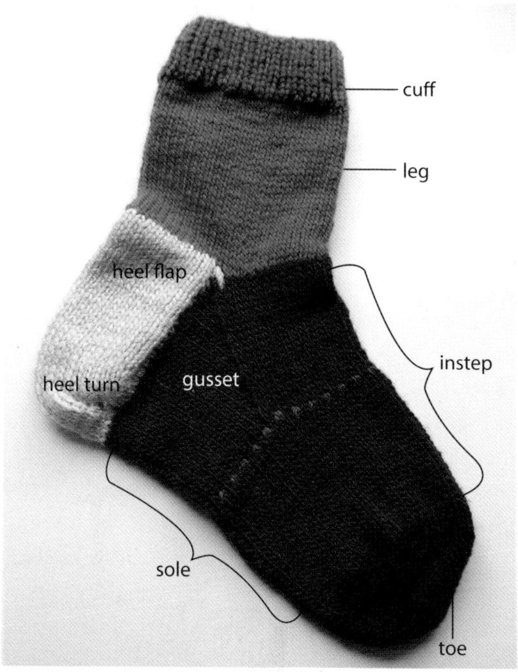

The different parts of a sock worked in different colours.

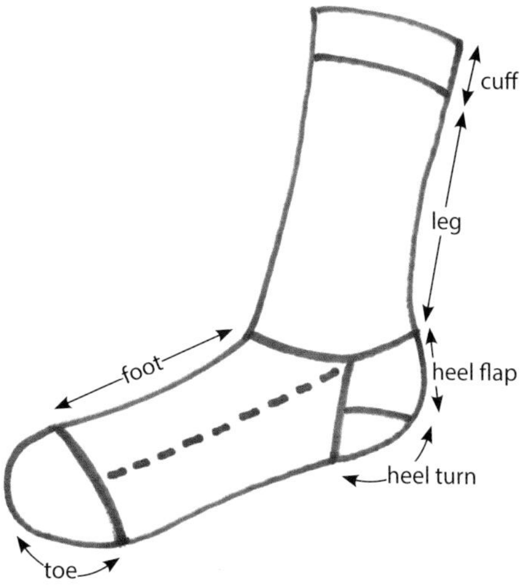

This diagram shows the important places to measure lengths to get the most comfortable and well-fitting sock.

The most accurate way to find the measurement of the under heel, sole and toe is to draw around the foot on a piece of card and mark the points at which the heel ends and the toe begins. This will also help to decide the best shape for knitting the toe as described in Chapter 4.

Ball of the foot

The first measurement to take is around the ball of the foot (i.e. the padded portion of the foot, between the toes and the arch). Measure at the point marked by the line of pale stitches on the purple section of the demonstration sock pictured on page 19. Take the measurement with a flexible tape measure and wrap it around exactly. Socks need to have a slight negative ease so that they don't fall down into the shoe. If you don't have a flexible tape measure, wrap a piece of yarn around the foot and then measure it along a fixed ruler.

In most cases the foot circumference will be the same as the leg circumference just above the ankle. In commercially made socks an average measurement for a woman's foot would be 21cm/8¼in; for a man's 24cm/9½in.

Leg and cuff

After taking the foot measurement, decide how long you want the leg of the sock to be and whereabouts the cuff will rest on the leg. Take the circumference of the leg at this point and then the length from the top of the cuff to the start of the heel. The standard leg length of a sock for women is around 16.5cm/6½in, for men around 2.5cm/1in more. Obviously, leg circumference varies a great deal and there is no standard size, so it is important to measure this accurately or the sock will either grip too tightly or not stay up. Measure around the leg at the point where the cast-on row of the cuff will sit. The number of stitches can be adjusted towards the ankle if necessary.

Heel height

The heel height from the top of the heel to the floor will normally be determined by the number of stitches in the leg for a short row heel. It is usually between 5cm/2in and 7cm/2¾in deep. However, it is possible to alter this length for a higher heel by working a few extra rows before starting the shaping. For a sock with a heel flap, which is normally worked as a square, make this section longer than it is wide, remembering that you will be picking up more stitches along the sides before working the gusset.

Foot length

The length of the foot will differ for each person. Measure the total foot length from the back of the heel to the tip of the big toe. The most accurate way to do this is to place the foot on a piece of card and draw around it. When you have taken this measurement subtract 10cm/4in or 5cm/2in for the heel and 5cm/2in for the toe. This will give you the length of knitting you need to do after the heel and before starting the toe shaping.

TENSION

When you have taken all of these measurements you will want to be sure that the knitting itself does actually comply with them. Don't just cast on and begin knitting; first make a swatch using the suggested yarn and needles. Written instructions will usually say whether the tension is for that of the pattern or for stocking stitch; the ball band of the yarn will almost always give the number of stitches and rows to 10cm/4in over stocking stitch. Before you start your sock, make a swatch about 5 or 6 inches square using the same needles that you will be using to knit your sock. Wash and block your swatch and then measure a 4-inch section in the middle of this swatch. Count the number of stitches and rows in this section and then compare them with the suggested number in the pattern. If there are fewer stitches and rows than recommended, try a smaller size needle; if there are more stitches and rows, use a larger needle. Ideally, because knit and purl rows sometimes behave slightly differently to each other, that is, some people knit purl rows more tightly than knit rows, or vice versa, it is best to knit your swatch in the round too.

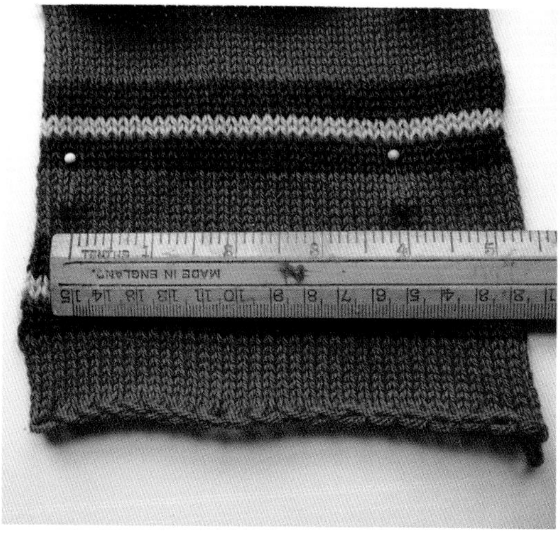

Measuring the stitch tension.

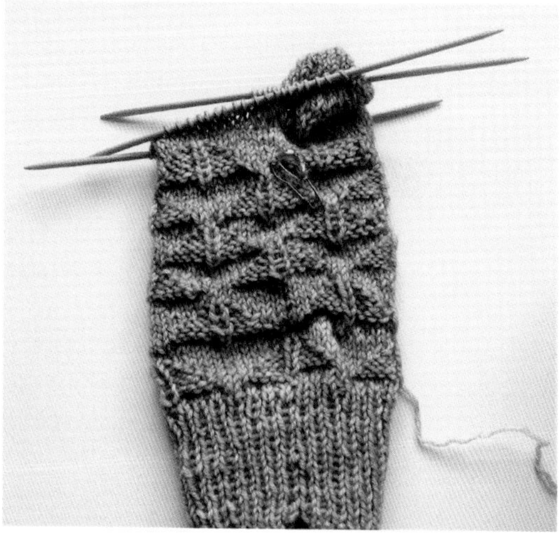

A stitch marker in place to mark the beginning of the round.

Once the stitch and row tension are established you can start knitting, either from the cuff down to the toe, or toe up to the cuff. Various methods of casting on for these two directions are described in the following sections.

KNITTING IN THE ROUND

Almost all socks are knitted in this way (also known as circular knitting), making a tube with a right-angled turn to shape the heel and then complete the foot. The work can be done using fixed or interchangeable circular needles, trio needles or sets of double-pointed needles. There will be no seams to rub on parts of the feet and nothing to sew up when the work is finished apart perhaps from a few grafted stitches at the tip of the toe. For the majority of the sock the right side of the work will be facing you as the work is never turned and is continually worked from right to left. For a plain sock it can all be completed using just the knit stitch, which is a special advantage where the sock is knitted in a colourwork pattern, as there is no need to reverse the placement of the motifs for a wrong side row. The only exceptions to this are the flap part of a heel, but as this section is often worked in a plain contrast colour it doesn't hinder the process, and where you might want to work in garter stitch. This entails working alternate rounds of knit and purl, the opposite to flat knitting where alternate rows of knit and purl produce stocking stitch and every row of knit creates garter stitch.

TIP

If working in knit two, purl two rib on double-pointed needles, the work is neater if the same pairs of stitches are not split over two needles.

Joining into a circle

When knitting in rounds, casting on is done in the same way as for straight needles; either casting all the stitches onto one needle and then dividing them onto three if using a set of double-pointed needles, or casting a third of the stitches onto each of the three needles. To make sure that all of the cast-on stitches lie in the same direction, lay the work down flat on a firm surface and pat them into position. making sure that none of the stitches are twisted over the needle and the edges formed by the cast on are all at the bottom of the needles.

To begin the work using a set of double-pointed needles, when all the stitches have been cast on to three needles, insert the empty working needle into the first cast on stitch, usually the slip knot, bring the needle with the last cast on stitch close to these tips and take the yarn around the working needle as firmly as possible so that it doesn't make a loop between the needles. Work around to the end of the round then continue working along each of the needles in turn dividing the stitches as evenly as possible over the three needles.

If using a circular needle, cast on all of the stitches as if using straight needles, then put the needle tips together, bringing the last stitch made close to the first one (again, usually the slip knot) and join the work by knitting into that first stitch, pulling the yarn quite firmly to avoid a loose thread and then pulling the next stitch tightly on the needle too.

Place a stitch marker at this point to mark the beginning of the round, or use a small piece of waste yarn, slipping it from the left tip to the right at the beginning of each round.

TIP

Cast on one more stitch than the required number. When joining the stitches for the first round, knit that extra stitch together with the first one to make a neat join.

COLOURWORK IN SOCKS

Stripes

The simplest way to bring colour into a pair of socks is to knit in stripes but knitting these in the round can make it appear that there is a little step from the end of the last round to the beginning of the next. This is because you are actually knitting in a spiral of a continuing round of stitches. The step is known as a 'jog' and there are ways of avoiding it.

Avoiding the 'jog'

1. Knit the required number of rows in your main colour.
2. Change to the contrast colour and knit one round.
3. At the beginning of the next round insert the tip of the needle into the first stitch of the last round of the main colour and lift it onto the left needle.
4. Knit it together with the first stitch of the new colour.

Alternatively, move the stitches on one place at the start of each round by slipping the first stitch of the new round instead of knitting it and joining the new colour after the slipped stitch.

Fair Isle

A plain pair of socks can be made more interesting by working them in a colour pattern or placing a band of Fair Isle around the leg or as a fold over cuff. The cable patterned cuff on Turnstone (*see* Chapter 5) could be replaced with one in stranded colourwork. Knitting socks with an all-over Fair Isle pattern can sometimes cause the socks to become too tight and inflexible because of the strands on the wrong side of the work. A way to avoid this is to keep pulling the newly created stitches back along the working needle, stretching out the floats at the back. Alternatively try catching in the contrast yarn on every third stitch, avoiding any floats longer than three stitches. Don't catch them in at the same place on each round though as this will start to show on the right side.

Another way to avoid the socks becoming too tight is to use needles one or two sizes larger for the coloured part and returning to the smaller needles for any plain section, or for the heels and toes. Or try knitting the socks inside out, so that the floats stretch around the outside of the circle instead of the shorter, inner side. Experiment with these techniques and see what works best for you and the pattern you're using.

Choosing colours

An important consideration when choosing colours for any stranded colour knitting is to make sure that there is a strong contrast between

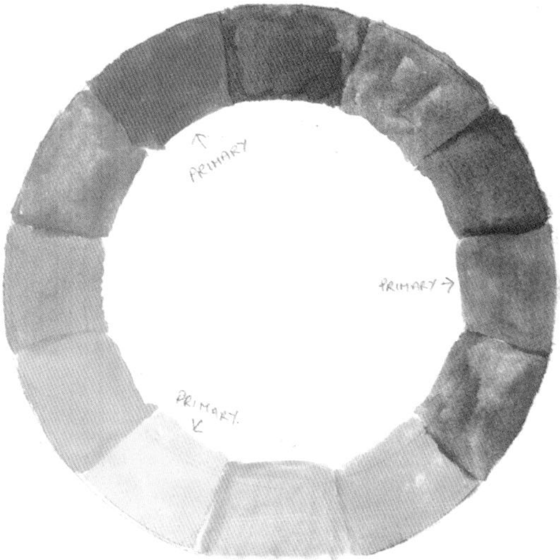

The primary colours on a colour wheel.

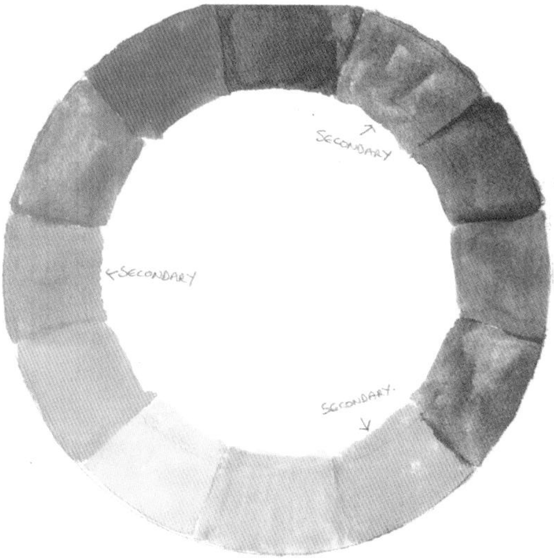

The secondary colours on a colour wheel.

them, especially those that are next to each other. Make sure that your darks are really darker than any of your light colours. Make yourself a colour wheel of the three primary colours – red, yellow and blue – and their secondary colours, that is, the ones you get by mixing two of the colours next to one another – orange, green and violet. Two colours from opposite sides of the colour wheel make a sharp contrast and invariably work well. Between the primary and secondary colours are a gradual range of colours moving through more red with just a hint of orange, to more orange with a little hint of red. Placing any of these adjacent colours next to one another will cause them to disappear into the fabric. A way to test whether similar colours will work is to photograph them in black and white and if you can't tell the difference between one and the next, they won't show up as a contrast in your knitting.

Colour dominance

When knitting Fair Isle or any stranded colour pattern, one colour will show up more than the other depending on how you carry the yarns. The colour that travels above the other will be less dominant as it does not have as far to travel as the one that moves down below the background colour and then back up again. Always keep the yarns in the same hands (or on the same fingers) to make sure that the correct colour is always the dominant one. When knitting two-handed, the dominant colour will be held in the left hand.

Following a chart in circular knitting

Some of the patterns in this book have charts. I have also included written instructions for those who think charts are difficult to follow but most of them are quite basic and can form a useful introduction to working from charts on other occasions. Because you are always knitting with the right side facing you in circular knitting, these charts are simpler to follow than those for flat knitting.

In each chart one square represents one stitch. The horizontal line of squares marks a whole row; you move up to the next line each time you get to the end of a round. Note that in some patterns a chart will only show every patterned round where alternate rounds are knitted plain but the charts in this book show every round. There are symbols for the way each stitch is knitted, for example in lace patterns a / means knit two together and an O stands for yarn over in order to make an eyelet hole.

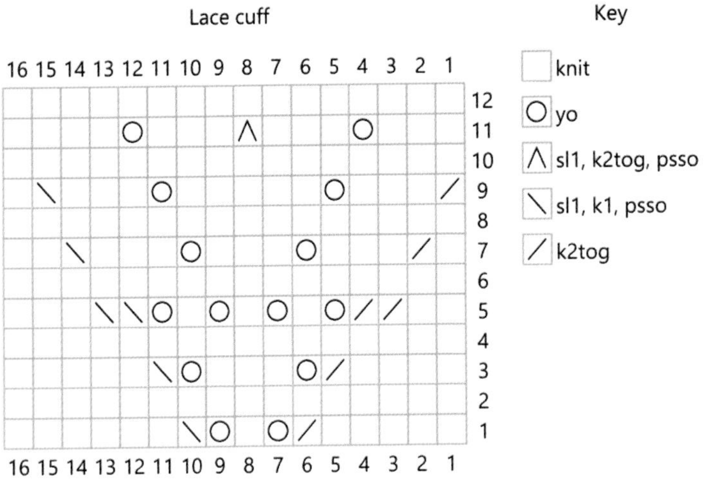

The knitting chart for the lace pattern on the Linnet socks – *see* Chapter 5.

The stitches are numbered along the bottom and the rows have numbers along the side of the chart; so the Linnet socks chart, pictured here, is a multiple of sixteen stitches and twelve rows. In row 1 you would knit five stitches then knit two together, make a yarn over to create the eyelet, knit 1, yarn over again, then slip 1, knit 1 and pass the slipped stitch over the knitted stitch to decrease one, then knit six more stitches. You would then repeat the chart from the first stitch again for as many times as required by the pattern. The second and each alternate row are all knit as denoted by the blank squares. When working in the round all of the rows are read from right to left.

Charts with cables may look slightly more complicated but it is a good idea to practice a cable chart a few times if you feel unsure of how to follow it. The Turnstone socks in Chapter 5 would be a good pattern to start with. The symbols for cables represent the direction in which the cable slopes. A pair of lines travelling from right to left means the cable will turn in that direction. A right to left twist is worked by slipping the required number of stitches onto a cable needle and leaving them at the front of the work while the next stitches are worked. The stitches from the cable needle are then worked as instructed. Sometimes there will be a dot within the cable symbol which means that one or two of the stitches are worked as purl(s). But a full explanation should be given in the key or the written instructions.

Charts for Fair Isle or other colourwork knitting often have the squares coloured in the actual colour of each stitch, but sometimes they use symbols instead. It is helpful to colour these in yourself using the colours that you have chosen for your project. Colourwork charts for circular knitting are almost exclusively worked as knit stitches throughout.

In all charts the stitches that are to be repeated across the row/round each time are usually outlined in a contrasting colour to the lines of the grid. If there are one or two extra stitches outside this box they denote those at the beginning and/or end of a row/round.

FIXING MISTAKES

Dropped stitches

If a stitch has slipped from the needle and been missed for a few rows it can be corrected by picking it up with a crochet hook. Slide the hook into the loop of the dropped stitch and then gradually work up the ladders between the stitches. If the dropped stitch is a long way down and the knitting becomes too tight as you do this it is probably better to undo the work to that point and start again.

Cable twisted in wrong direction

If an incorrect twist is noticed just a few rows down it can be corrected by dropping the stitches and then picking them up as above in the correct position. If the mistake was not noticed until much later it can sometimes be disguised by embroidering stitches in Swiss darning over it sloping in the correct direction.

CONSTRUCTION DETAILS FOR CUFF DOWN SOCKS

The cuff down way of working socks is the traditional Western way. Once the correct number of stitches is cast on it is easy to work out how many are required for the various sections; the foot usually has the same number of stitches as the number above the ankle, the heel or the heel flap starts with half of that number and the heel is turned over two thirds of those stitches. These numbers can, of course, be changed for wide or narrow heels, which is why it is essential to take accurate measurements and then calculate the width required based on your gauge swatch.

Cuff down knitting has the advantage that after knitting two or three rounds it is easy to tell if the cuff will fit snugly around the calf or will be too tight and difficult to get on. Too loose and it will not stay up but will gather around the ankle. It is easier to undo this short section and start again, rather than having to work out increases or decreases while working the leg and possibly disrupting a pattern.

Working from the top down has the slight disadvantage that you could run out of yarn before finishing the second sock, especially if you have made the leg longer than a pattern suggested. It is possible to remove a few rows of knitting from the top but it can be a bit fiddly, especially if the socks are patterned.

One way to overcome this is to divide your yarn into two equal portions before starting to knit. Read the weight from the label or weigh the skein then wind off what appears to be half of it. Weigh the ball that you have wound and if it is not half of the original skein either wind a bit more or unwind some and weigh it again. When it is half of the original weight, break off the yarn and wind the rest of the skein into the second ball.

Casting on

The majority of printed patterns will say 'cast on # stitches' without indicating which method to use, assuming that the knitter will use the one they are most familiar with. But the different methods produce slightly different results, and it is worth experimenting to see which one suits the project best. Below are some suggestions of various ways to cast on for a cuff-down sock.

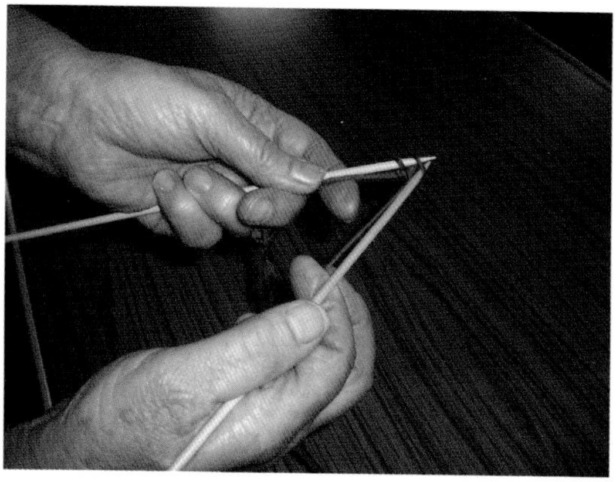

Step 1: Make a slip knot and place it on the left needle. Insert the right needle up through the front loop.

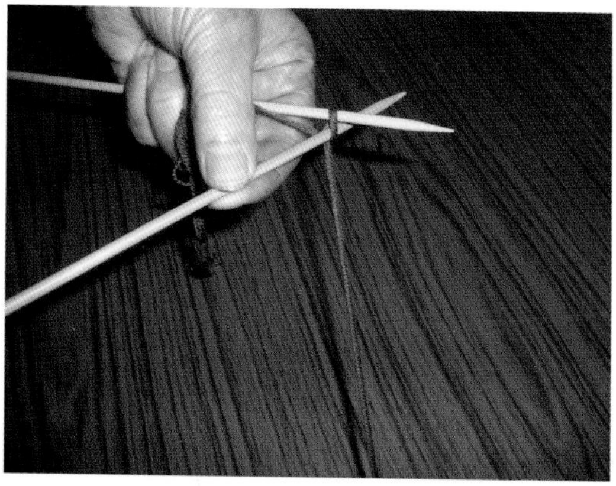

Step 2: Take the yarn anti-clockwise around the needle.

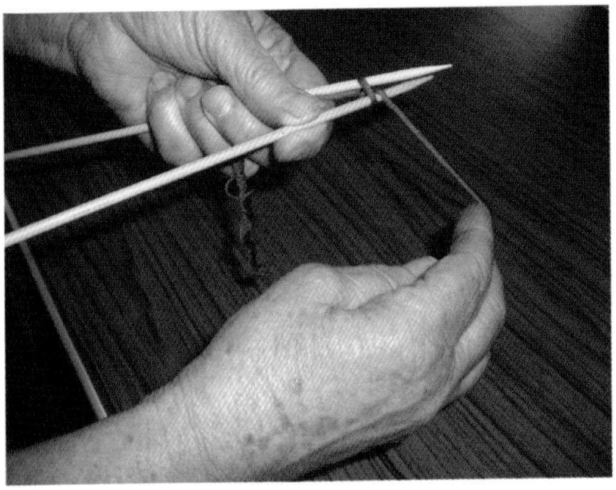

Step 3: Bring the needle down and forwards making a loop.

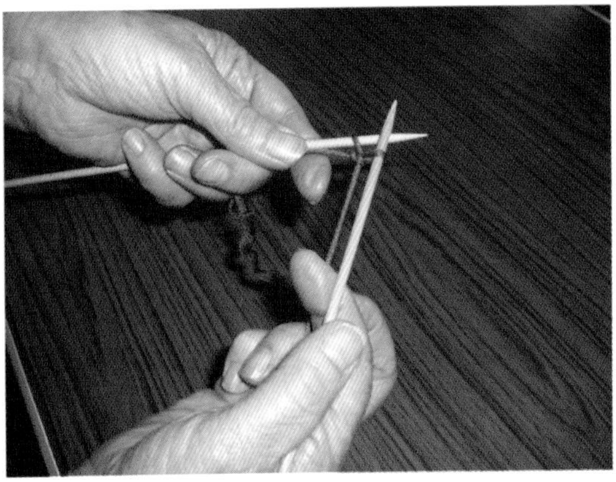

Step 4: Place the loop on the left needle.

Knit cast on and cable cast on

These two methods are probably the ones that are automatically chosen by most people when they begin to knit. They are usually taught to children when they first learn to knit as they are made in the same way as the basic knit stitch. They are the methods most knitters turn to first and then, from habit, continue to use. But there are other methods, some more useful and more stretchy than others, so better suited to sock knitting.

Working into the loops is knit cast on; working between the loops is referred to as a cable cast on.

For a neat edge to a ribbed cuff, try casting on alternately knitwise and purlwise using either of the two techniques.

TIP

In flat knitting when the required number of stitches are cast on and the tail end of yarn is on the left, there will be a row of slanting loops at the base. When the work is turned to start knitting the base row will be a row of ridges like those on the reverse side of stocking stitch. If you are working the next few rows in garter stitch this can be an advantage as it resembles the other rows. But if you don't want the ridges on the right side of the work, begin your knitting with a purl row. When working in the round the slanting loops will be on the right side and the ridges on the inside.

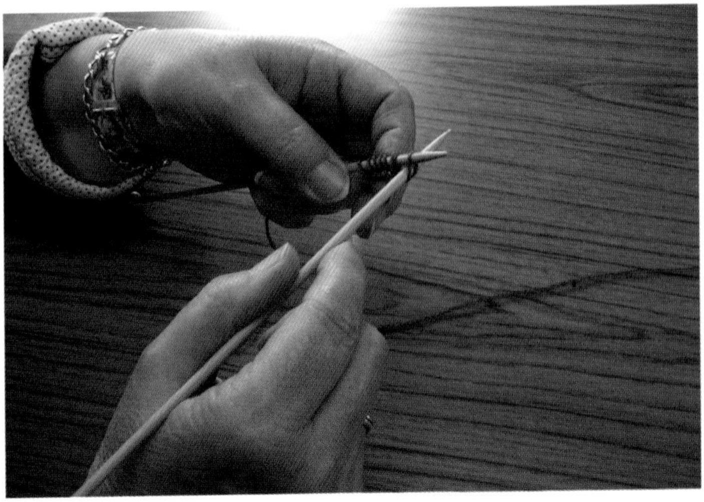

Cable cast on.

Long tail or thumb cast on

This is quite a flexible cast on that works well for garter stitch or ribbed cuffs.

Measure a length of yarn about four times the length of your cuff circumference or approximately 2cm for each stitch and fold it back on itself.

Repeat steps 2 to 4 for the number of stitches required.

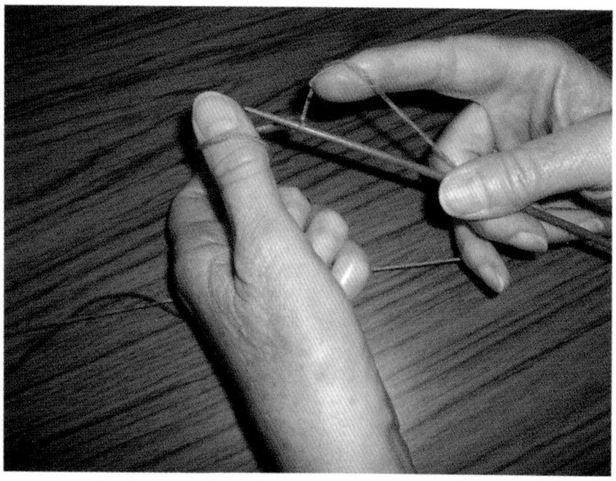

Step 1: Make a slip knot at the fold and place it on the needle. Wrap the tail end of the yarn around the back of your thumb to the front, i.e. anti-clockwise.

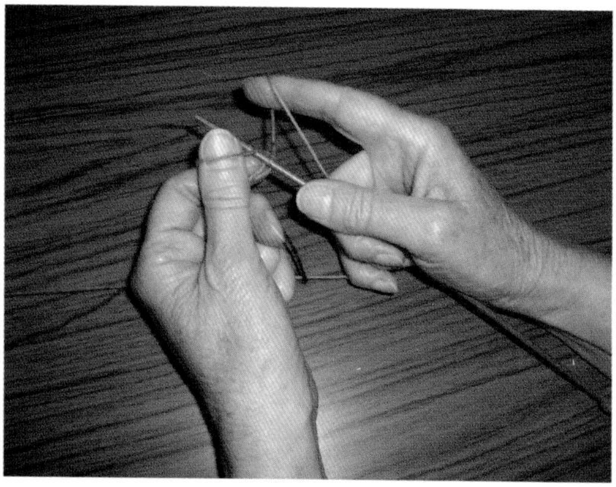

Step 2: Insert the needle under the strand at the front so that it comes up through the centre of the loop, from the bottom of the thumb towards the top.

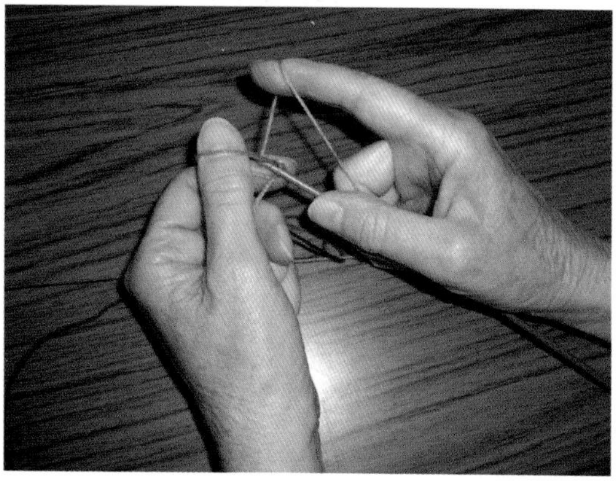

Step 3: Take the yarn from the ball around the needle and bring the needle down through the loop on the thumb.

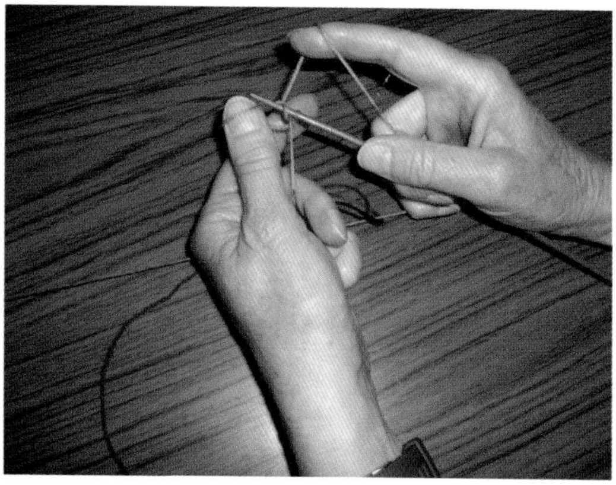

Step 4: Slide your thumb out of the loop and pull the yarn so that the new stitch tightens up (but not too tightly) on the needle.

Old Norwegian cast on

The slightly more complex method, sometimes known as Old Norwegian cast on or German twisted cast on entails holding both ends of yarn in the hand. It makes a slightly more stretchy and decorative edge. Again, only one needle is used.

Repeat from step 2.

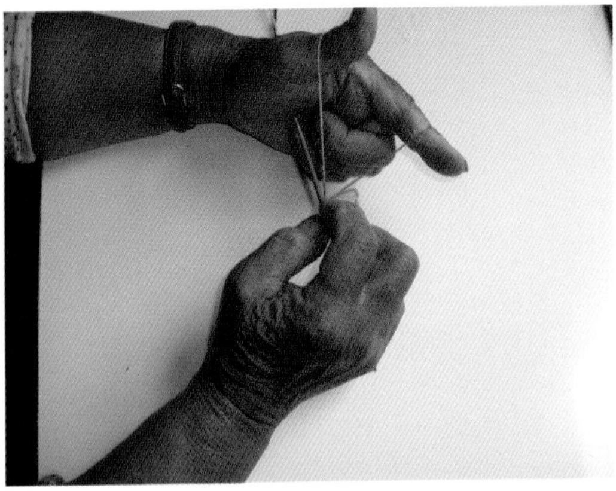

Step 1: Place a slipknot on the needle, hold the two strands of the yarn firmly in your palm. Place the thumb and index finger of your left hand between the yarn ends so that the tail end is around the thumb and the strand attached to the ball is over the index finger.

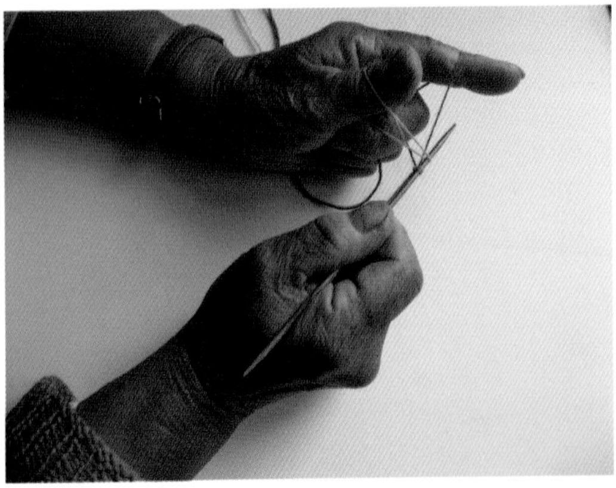

Step 2: Take the needle under both strands of yarn around the thumb, and then down from top to bottom into the centre of the thumb loop.

TIP

In the Old Norwegian cast on, to prevent the cast-on edge being too tight, it can be helpful to use a needle one size larger.

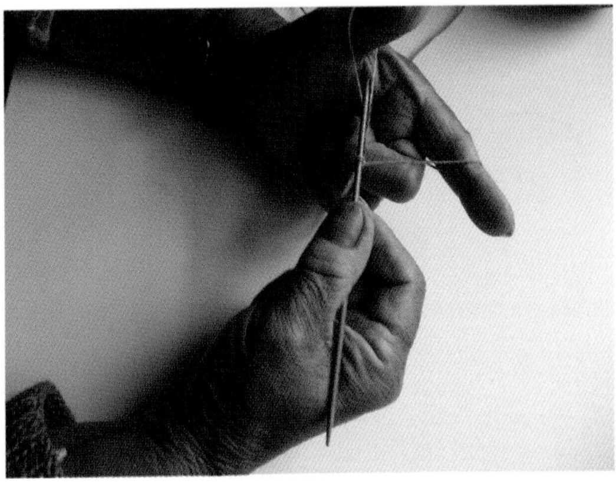

Step 3: Bring the needle forward so that the yarn on the thumb is twisted.

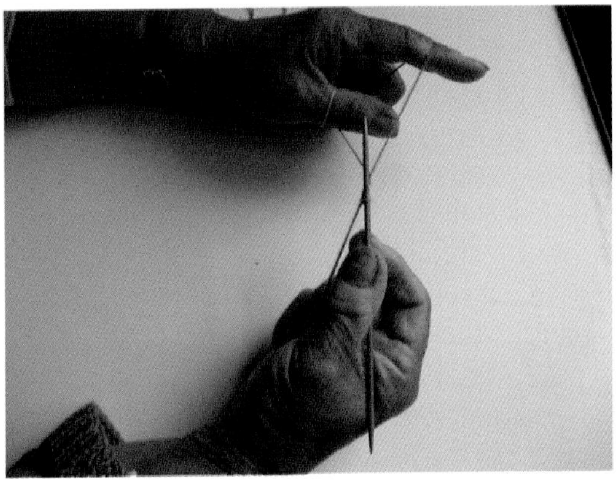

Step 4: Go over the thumb loop and under the loop on the index finger.

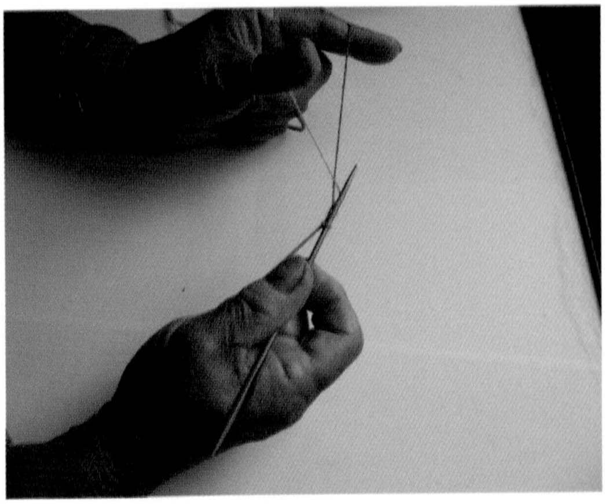

Step 5: Bring the needle back down through the bottom part of the thumb loop, below where the strands crossed.

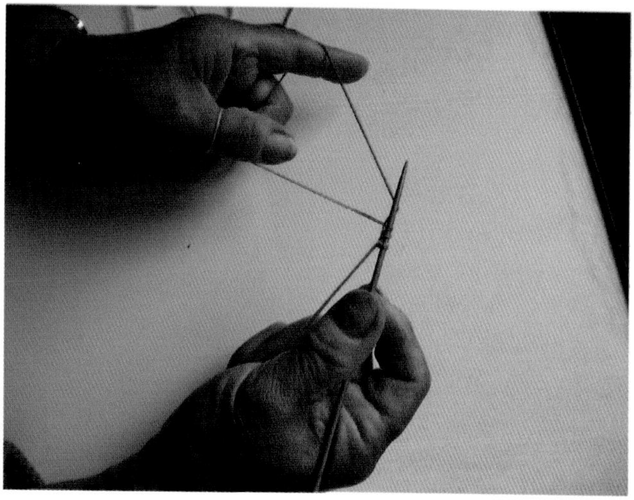

Step 6: Drop the loop off your thumb, tightening up the resulting stitch on the needle.

Yarn over cast on

This makes a fairly open edge that is easier to pick up stitches from if working a lace cuff. It is not so good on its own, however, as it tends to curl over.

Repeat steps 2 to 4 for the number of stitches required, inserting the needle between the yarn over and the stitch just made. The yarn overs count as a stitch.

TIP

The Yarn Over cast on is useful if you want to add a lace edging to the top of your sock as it is easy to pick up from.

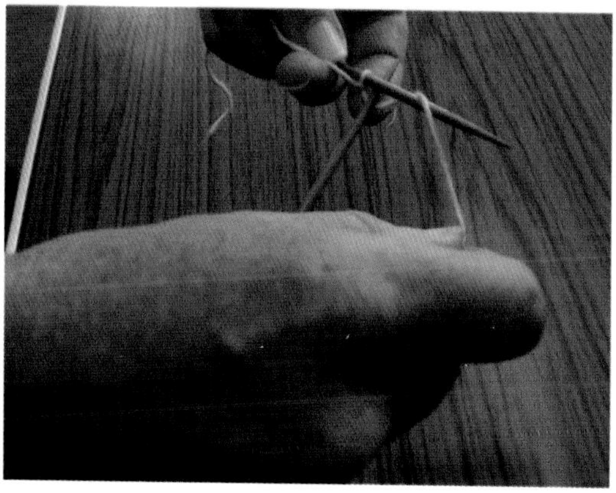

Step 3: insert the right-hand needle between the slip knot and the yarn over.

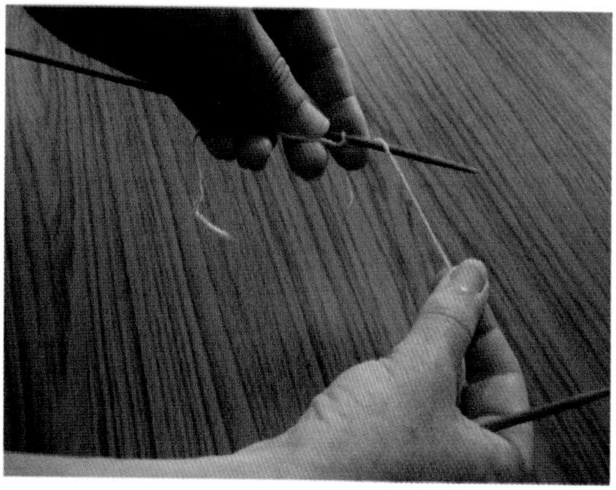

Step 1: Make a slip knot near the end of the yarn and place it on the left-hand needle.
Step 2: Take the yarn over the left tip from back to front.

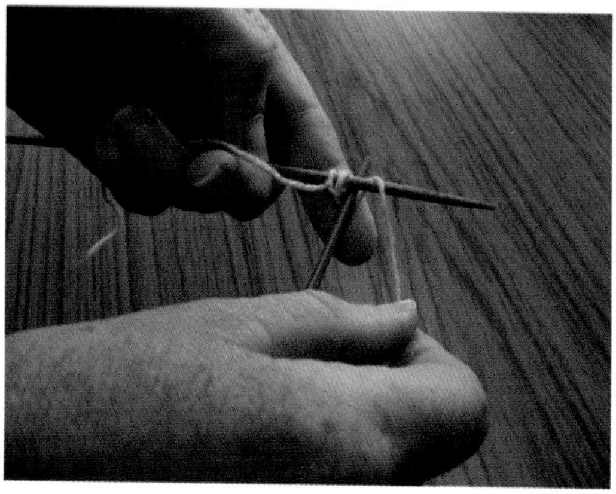

Step 4: Take the yarn around the right needle tip and pull it through between the stitches. Place this new stitch on the left-hand needle

Folded hem with picot edge

A pretty edge, often used with a lace pattern. It also gives a soft top to the cuff.

1. Cast on the required number of stitches using your preferred method and working fairly loosely.
2. Knit about 5 rows.
3. K1 (yf, k2tog) to end.
4. Knit one row less than in step 2.
5. Fold the knitting in half.
6. Slip the RH needle under the first cast-on stitch and knit it together with the stitch on the needle.
7. Knit the next stitch on the needle as normal.
8. Slip the needle under the 3rd cast-on stitch and knit together with the stitch on the needle.

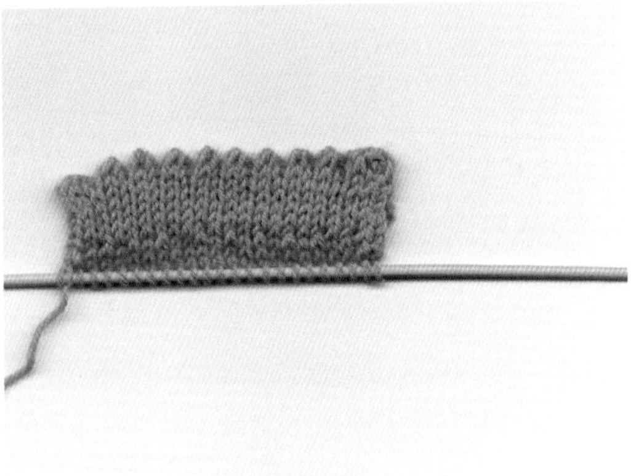

Folded picot edge making a soft top to the cuff.

TIP

Knitting together alternate stitches instead of every stitch helps to make the picot edge lie flatter.

TIP

When knitting in the round, be careful not to twist the stitches before joining the ring. It is easiest to work all the stitches onto one needle then work a row or two before joining them. Sew up the small gap that has occurred when all the work is finished.

Two-colour cast on

This is best worked as a long-tail cast on, but using two different coloured yarns. It makes a neat edging for cuffs worked in corrugated rib but is also an attractive edge in its own right.

Make the slip knot with both ends of yarn held together, and place one colour on your index finger and the other one on your thumb. Work exactly as long-tail cast on and you will see that the yarn on the thumb carries a line of colour below the stitches made by the yarn on your index finger.

Various cuffs

Once the cast-on row is completed there are a number of ways to complete the cuffs:

- Knit 1 purl 1 rib (not as elastic as other ribs) over an even number of stitches. This is the rib most often used.
- Knit 2 purl 2 rib uses a multiple of 4 stitches and is more elastic than knit 1 purl 1 rib.
- Twin rib is a multiple of 6 stitches.

Each of these methods will feature in at least one of the patterns in this book.

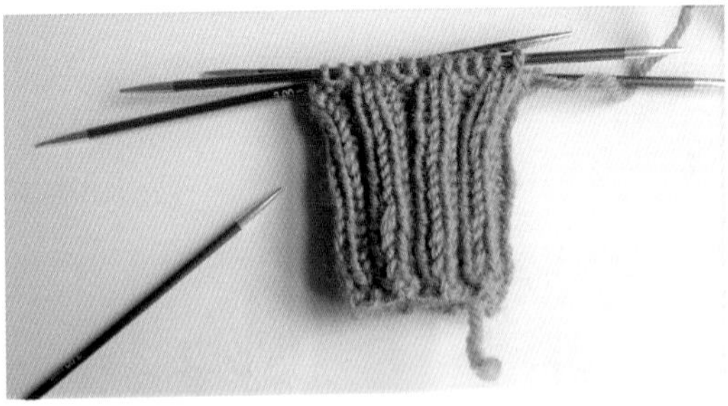

Knit 2 purl 2 rib.

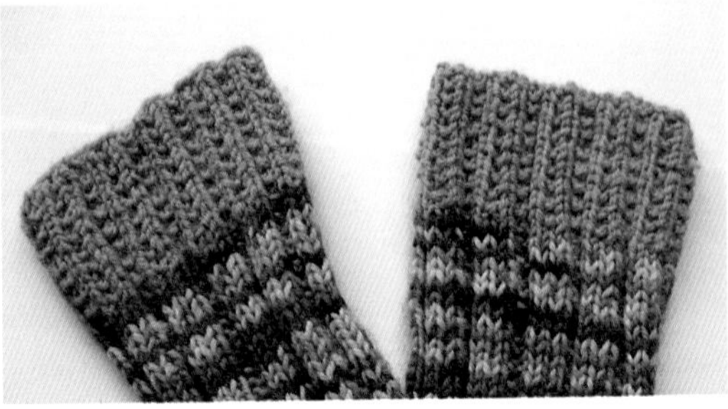

Twin rib, as used in the Mallard Socks.

Rolled edge cuff

A rolled edge cuff will not grip the leg as well as a ribbed cuff, so usually has a few rows of ribbing after the edge has been worked.

1. Cast on the required number of stitches with one size larger needle.
2. Knit at least 5 rounds.
3. Change to smaller needles and either work a few rounds of rib or begin the pattern. The cuff will roll back so that the wrong side is showing.

Sideways cuff

This cuff gives an accurate fit for a sock without having to work out the number of stitches. The Partridge sock in Chapter 5 is knitted with a sideways cuff.

1. Using the same-sized needle you plan to use for the whole sock, cast on about 15 stitches (this will give a cuff approximately two inches deep). If you wish to graft the ends together, use one of the provisional cast-on methods.
2. Knit in garter stitch until the cuff will fit snugly around the ankle.
3. Join the cast-on and cast-off edges together, either by grafting or sewing them together on the wrong side.

Picking up one stitch for each ridge of the garter stitch should give you the correct number of stitches to begin the leg. An interesting cuff can be made by working this in rows of stripes.

TIP

A lace edge could be added to the sideways cuff by picking up stitches along the top edge.

Decorative tops

The cuffs of a sock can be knitted sideways, to add cabled tops or pretty lace edgings. For example, the Turnstone sock is started with a cabled cuff (see Chapter 5).

Lace edgings can also be added to the top of a sock after the work is finished. They can be worked in the opposite direction to the sock by starting the work with a provisional cast on. The Linnet socks are worked in this way (see Chapter 5).

Provisional cast on

This method requires a length of waste yarn as well as the working yarn. It is useful where a lace cuff or alternative top is required after the main part is finished..

1. Hold a length of waste yarn below the needle and around the left thumb.
2. Hold the working yarn over the left index finger.
3. Bring the needle forwards under the waste yarn and over the top of the working yarn.
4. Bring the working yarn in front of the waste yarn to make 1 stitch.
5. For the next stitch, take the needle over the top of the waste yarn, behind the working yarn.
6. Bring the working yarn forwards and repeat for the required number of stitches.

To add a lace edging worked in the opposite direction to the cuff, slide the working yarn stitches onto a smaller needle before removing any waste yarn from a provisional cast on.

After the leg is knitted in your chosen pattern it is time to knit the heel. Again, there are a number of different heel designs, and these will be described in Chapter 3. There are different methods for working the heels on a cuff down or toe up sock, although the methods of working short row heels are the same whichever direction

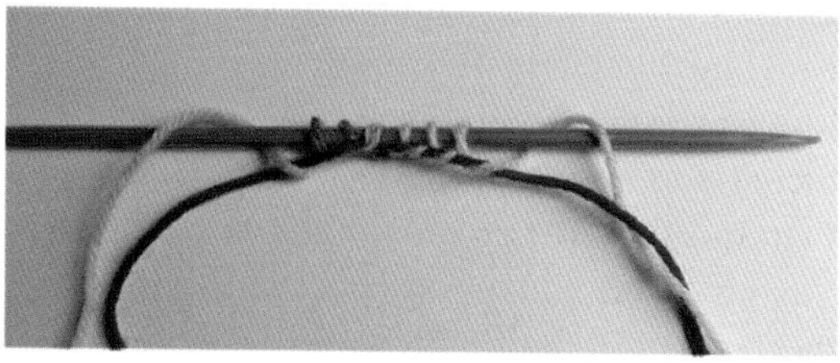

The red yarn is the waste yarn used for a provisional cast on.

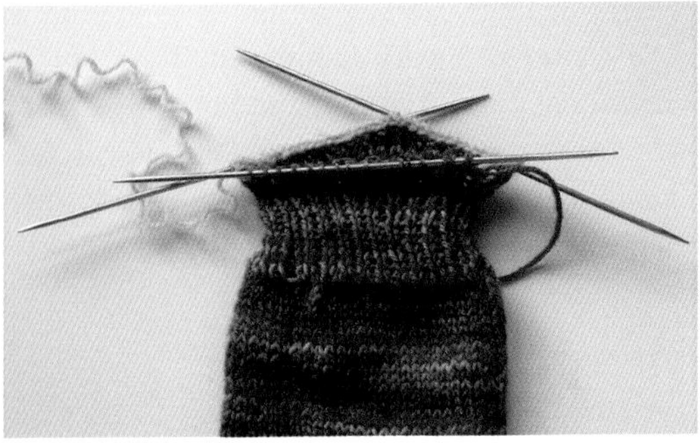

Gradually undoing the waste yarn while picking up the live stitches to knit a lace cuff.

the sock is knitted. There are also various ways of casting off at the end of a toe up sock.

TOE UP CONSTRUCTION METHODS

Working a sock from the toe up has the advantage of making it easy to adjust the fit by trying it on as you knit. This is naturally easier when working on a long circular needle, but it can be done carefully with a set of double pointed needles. Another advantage is that the length of leg is easy to adjust if there is only a limited amount of yarn.

A disadvantage is that casting on to begin the closed toe can be a bit awkward at first.

Beginning the toe

When working toe up socks it is necessary to increase after the initial cast-on row. For a round toe for example: cast on 8 stitches, 4 on each of the 2 circular needles or 2 on each of 4 double-pointed needles or if working on three dpns, 3 on 2 needles and 2 on the 3rd needle. Knit one round on these 8 stitches, then increase in every stitch. Knit 1 round more, and then increase in every alternate stitch. Knit 1 round then increase in every third stitch; continue in this way, working one more stitch between the increases until there are the required number of stitches.

TIP

Thread the yarn through the stitches of the cast-on row several times to close up the small hole that sometimes occurs.

Other ways of starting the toes are described in Chapter 4.

Casting off at the cuff for toe up socks

The cast-off row can sometimes end up rather tight. Either use needles a size larger or try one of the more stretchy cast offs described below.

Casting off knitwise

This is the traditional cast off, which serves well for most purposes but can look unsuitable for a ribbed edge.

1. Knit 2 stitches.
2. Pass the first of these over the second.
3. Knit the next stitch.
4. Pass the stitch to the right over it and off the needle.
5. Continue in this way until all stitches have been cast off. Cut off the yarn and pass the end through the last stitch.

Casting off purlwise

Worked in the same way as the knitwise cast off but using purl stitches. It forms a ridge when worked on the right side but if worked from the wrong side the right side will look the same as for a knitwise cast off.

Casting off over ribbed stitches

This is worked in a combination of the above two methods, working the stitches as set by the rib pattern.

Stretchy cast off

1. Knit the first two stitches.
2. Slip them back to the left needle.
3. Knit them together through the back loops.

4. Knit the next stitch and slip it and the stitch already on the needle back to the left needle.
5. Continue in this way until all stitches are worked off.

Icelandic cast off

This is a very flexible edge, even more so than the stretchy cast off. It is useful for finishing off a lace pattern as it will lie flat when blocked.

1. K1, slip this stitch purlwise onto the left needle.
2. Insert right needle purlwise into first stitch and knitwise into second.
3. Pull second stitch back through first.
4. Repeat steps 2 and 3.
5. When all stitches are worked off, fasten the tail end through the last stitch and weave in down the inside of the sock.

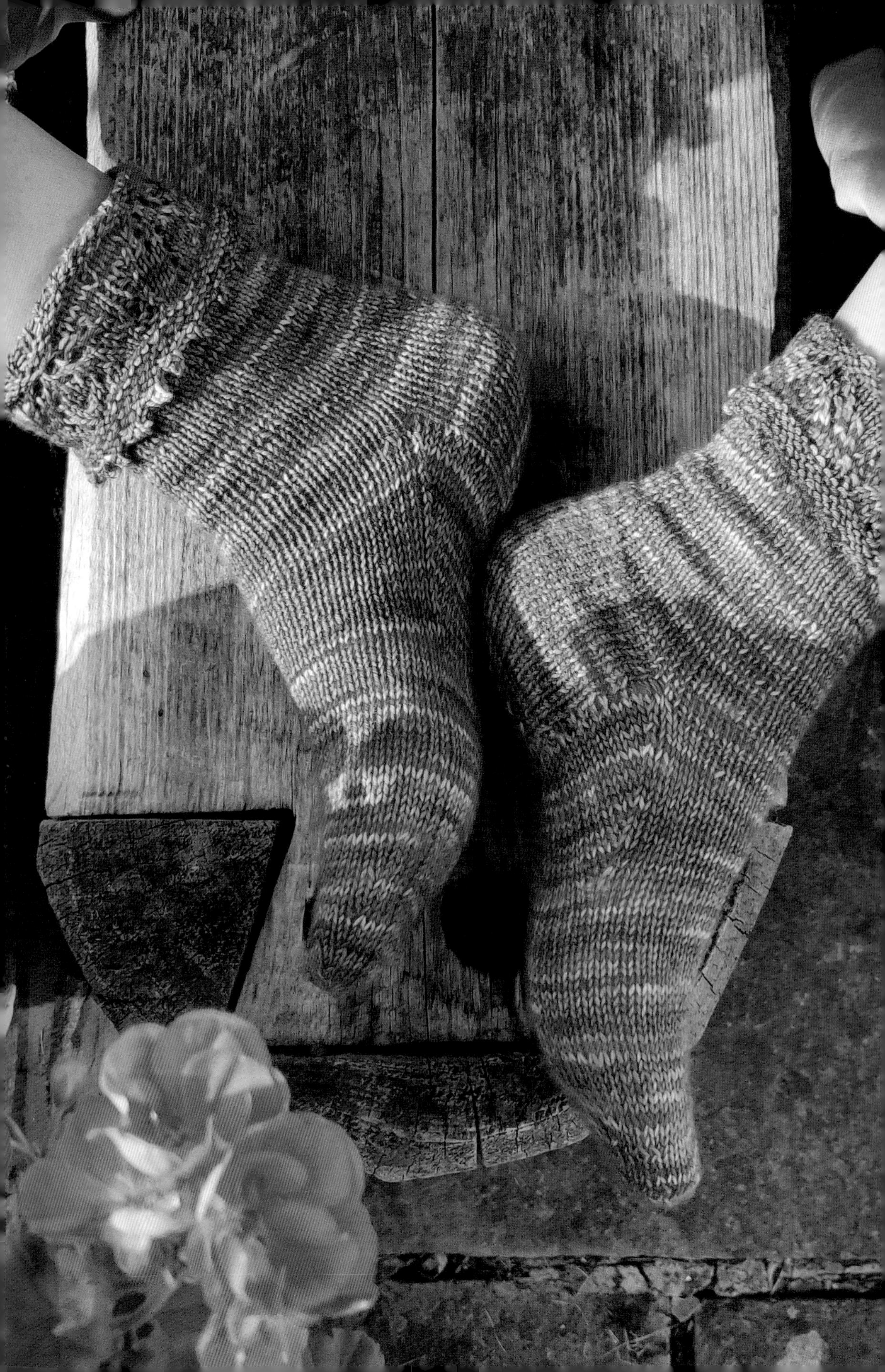

CHAPTER 3

Heels

When stockings were made from cloth they had to be cut and seamed into shape to create the foot. But the flexibility of knitting means that the sock can be worked in one piece as a long tube with stitches manipulated to form the bend that will lead into the foot. This bend is to turn the fabric ready to create the foot as well as to accommodate the heel. There are two ways to make the bend: as a rectangular heel flap with a gusset or as a series of short rows.

To make sure that your heel fits comfortably in the sock, measure the height of the heel from the floor to the highest part of the heel. If following a printed pattern with a heel flap and gusset and this seems too shallow for you, a few extra rows can be worked in the heel flap if necessary. Remember to pick up extra stitches along the sides if you have lengthened the flap. One stitch picked up for each of the slipped stitches at the start of each row will give the correct measurement. For a high heel worked top down over short rows, work a few rows straight before starting the shaping.

There are a number of ways of working short row heels and some of them are described in this chapter.

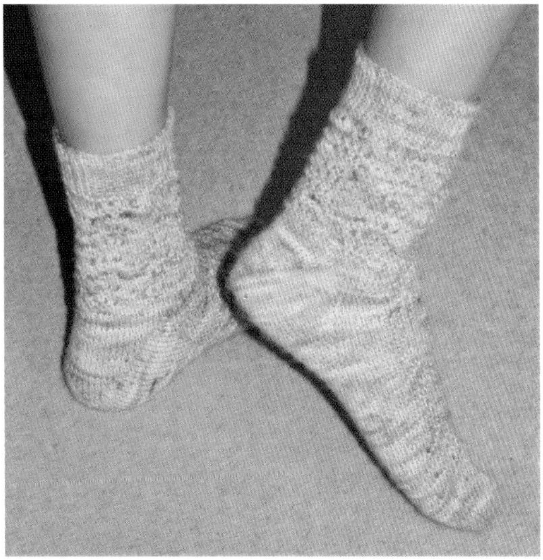

The Fleegle heels on the Serin socks.

SHORT ROW HEELS

The short row shaped heel resembles that of a commercially made sock produced on a machine. Removing and holding stitches to create a separate flap and gusset would be awkward and time consuming on a machine, necessitating the removal of stitches and then rehanging them on the needles after completing the shaping. Consequently, an alternative method was devised in which some stitches could be left on the needles unworked, then returned to working to form a 'cup' for the heel. When this is done by hand, leaving stitches unworked to pick up from later can leave a hole. So various ways have been devised to make this hole less noticeable or to try to close it altogether.

The following methods of working partial rows before turning and completing all of the stitches can be used for socks worked from the cuff down or toe up. The heel is created in the same way for either direction. The most frequently used method involves wrapping the yarn around each of the approaching stitches on the needle.

Basic 'wrap and turn' method (w&t)

To wrap a stitch, take the yarn around the following stitch then bring it back to the appropriate working position, i.e., to the back for the next knit stitch, or to the front for the next purl stitch.

Row 1 (RS): k to last stitch, wrap the last stitch and turn ready to purl the next stitch.
Row 2 (WS): p to last stitch, wrap the last stitch and turn ready to knit the next stitch.
Row 3: k to the stitch before the first wrapped stitch, w&t.
Row 4: p to stitch before the first wrapped stitch, w&t.

Repeat rows 3 and 4 until one third of the stitches are wrapped on each side of the unwrapped centre stitches.

The second part of the heel widens it back again.

Row 1 (RS): sl1, k to first wrapped stitch, work wrap and next stitch together, w&t the following stitch (this stitch will now have two wraps).
Row 2 (WS): sl1, p to first wrapped stitch, work wrap and next stitch together, w&t (this stitch will now have two wraps).
Row 3: sl1, k to next wrapped stitch, work both wraps and next stitch together, w&t (this stitch will now have two wraps).
Row 4: sl1, p to next wrapped stitch, work both wrap and next stitch together, w&t (this stitch will now have two wraps).

Repeat rows 3 and 4 until you have one wrapped stitch on each side.

Next row: sl1, k to last wrapped stitch, work wrap and next stitch together.

Next row: sl1, k to last wrapped stitch, work wrap and next stitch together.

Join the work to continue in the round, work across instep, work wrap and stitch together, k to end of round.

Shadow wraps

This method produces a pair of legs to each stitch that is to be left unworked.

1. Work to the last two stitches on the needle. Insert the tip of the right needle into the stitch of the row below and place it on the left needle.
2. Knit into that new stitch so that it is now on the right-hand needle.
3. Slip the original stitch from the left needle next to the new stitch on the right-hand needle.
4. Turn and slip this double stitch before working to the opposite end.
5. Lift the stitch of the row below onto the right-hand needle and purl it together with the original stitch.

Repeat these two rows until there are approximately one third of stitches left at the centre. Work across all of the first half of stitches, treating each of the double stitches as though they were one stitch. Work across the rest of the stitches to complete the heel.

Slip stitch method

This is the simplest way to work short rows but it can create large stitches if the yarn is not pulled tight.

1. Knit as far as the last stitch; turn, slip the next stitch and pull on the yarn to tighten it, purl the next stitch and tighten that too.
2. Work to the last stitch of the following row and repeat, slipping, tightening, working the next stitch and tightening that too.

When working back over the stitches, tighten the slipped ones again and this should avoid a hole.

Mock short rows

This method actually involves decreasing and picking up stitches, rather than leaving stitches unworked.

1. Begin by dividing your stitches into thirds and place markers at the dividing points.
2. Knit to two stitches before the end and knit them together.
3. Purl to two stitches before the end and purl them together.
4. Repeat these two rows as far as the markers.
5. Knit across the centre stitches then pick up and knit a stitch from the first decreased stitch.
6. Purl across the centre stitches, pick up and purl a stitch from the decreased stitches.

Repeat these two rows until the stitches are back to their original number.

German short rows

This method looks as though two stitches have been made from one, but all it involves is to pull each unworked stitch tightly so that both legs lie on the needle.

1. Work two rows across all stitches, still pulling the last stitch of each row tightly.
2. On the return section work through the doubled stitches as though knitting/purling two together and continue to make the double stitches as before on the last stitch of each row.
3. Work two thirds of the stitches, make a double stitch, work half of these stitches and make a double stitch, then continue to work one more stitch each time, still pulling on the next stitch before the turn. For example, on a sock with 56 stitches, work 27 for the heel, pull the next stitch firmly and turn; purl 26 stitches, pull the next one firmly and turn.
4. Continue in this manner until there are 8 stitches left in the centre.
5. Work 2 rows across all stitches. Knit 17, pull the next one firmly and turn; purl 8, pull the next one firmly and turn.
6. Continue working to the doubled stitch of each row, pulling on the one before it, turn and work to next doubled stitch until all the stitches are back working.

Fish Lips Kiss Heel

This is a method devised by Patty Joy White and the instructions are her copyright. They are available for $1 from www.ravelry.com.

The technique requires a cardboard template of the foot and needs accurate measurements. It uses short row shaping that starts precisely at the point of the ankle bone for toe up socks. For cuff down socks this means knitting a further one inch of leg before starting the shaping and for toe up socks, knitting an extra inch after the shaping is completed. To work the short rows Patty suggests tightening the yarn so that both legs of the stitch are on the needle as in German short rows; she refers to this as a twin stitch, which is knitted as one stitch on the return row.

SQUARE HEELS

Each of these heels has a length of flat knitting, a turning section and a gusset with decreases narrowing the number of stitches down to fit the circumference of the foot.

The heel flap is knitted flat on two needles over half of the number of stitches in the sock, or, if decreases were made over the calf, in that section around the ankle. The other half of the

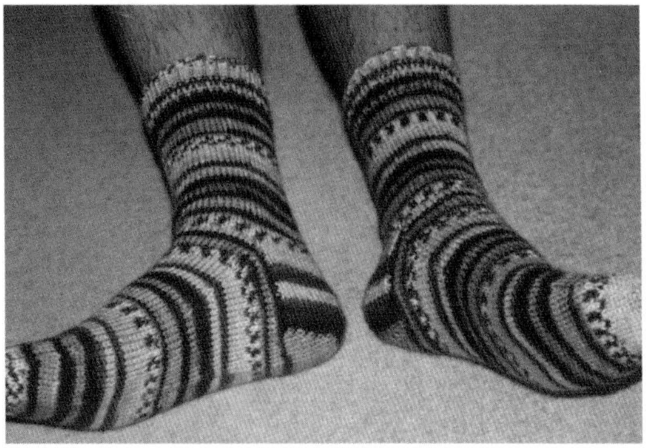

The French heels on the Jay socks.

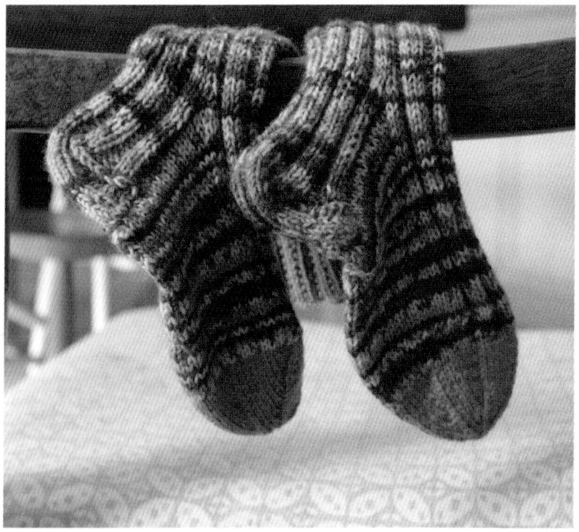

The ribbed heels on the Mallard socks.

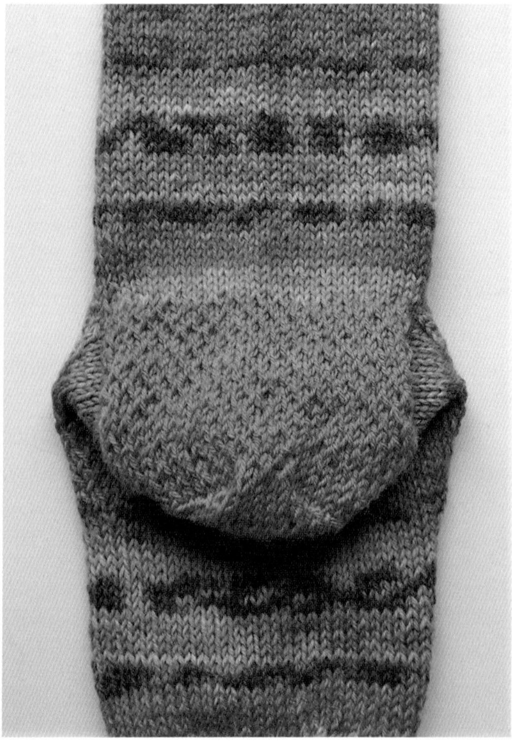

The Eye of Partridge heel in the Partridge socks.

stitches are left on a spare needle for the instep. So, if your sock has been worked on 60 stitches you would leave 30 on the needle(s) for the instep and work the flap on 30 stitches. The turning section is worked over approximately one third of the stitches in the heel flap, 10 stitches in this case, and can be shaped in a variety of ways.

The basic heel flap is knitted in stocking stitch with a slipped stitch at the beginning of every row to be picked up later for the gusset. There is no reason why the heel flap could not be knitted in pattern or any other variety of stitches; the Mallard pattern in Chapter 5 has a ribbed heel flap. A slipped stitch pattern, such as Eye of Partridge used in the Partridge pattern in Chapter 5, makes a slightly harder wearing, but still soft and comfortable, heel.

While the heel flap is usually knitted as a square, the turning section can be worked in a number of different ways.

Dutch heel

After dividing the stitches into two sections, half for the heel and half for the instep, leave the instep stitches on spare needles and work the heel flap. This heel is very square and box like.

Row 1: sl1, k two thirds of the heel stitches, ssk and turn.
Row 2: sl1, p one third of the heel stitches, p2tog and turn.
Row 3: sl1, k one third of the heel stitches, ssk and turn.

Repeat the last 2 rows until all stitches have been worked.

Rounded heel

As for Row 1 of the square heel, but then work one more stitch on each row after the decrease.

Example over 60 stitches.

Row 1: sl1, k16, ssk, k1, turn.
Row 2: sl1, p5, p2tog, p1, turn.
Row 3: sl1, k6, ssk, k1, turn.
Row 4: sl1, p7, p2tog, p1, turn.

Continue in this way until all stitches have been worked.

Triangular or French heel

Example over 60 stitches.

Row 1: sl1, k14, ssk, k1, turn.
Row 2: sl1, p1, p2tog, turn.
Row 3: sl1, k2, ssk, turn.
Row 4: sl1, p3, p2tog, turn.

And so on, working one more stitch between decreases until all the stitches have been worked.

Each sock in the pattern chapter will describe which form of shaping is used and how many stitches to work before decreasing.

Pick up and knit

After working a heel flap and turning section it is necessary to pick up stitches along the sides and then work a shaped gusset to return to the original number of stitches for the foot.

If your heel is worked in stocking stitch, slide the tip of the needle under both strands of the first stitch one in from the edge. Wrap the yarn around the needle and slide it forwards to make a stitch. Continue in this way along all of the edge stitches. If in the unlikely event that you have knitted your heel in garter stitch insert the tip of the needle through the lines between the bumps of stitches that mark each ridge.

Knit across the stitches remaining in the turned section of the heel, then pick up one stitch for each of the slipped stitches along the side of the flap; knit across the instep stitches left on the spare needle then pick up each of the slipped stitches on the other sides of the heel flap. The gusset is usually shaped by decreasing one stitch at each side of the heel stitches on alternate rounds. It can be helpful to place a stitch marker at the points where the instep stitches begin and end and then make the decreases before and after the markers.

Afterthought heels

This is a useful technique for working heels in a contrast colour, or for working with self-striping yarn where you don't want the pattern broken up. It is formed by working half of the stitches in a waste yarn that will be removed when the stitches are picked up for the heel. The sock is worked as a straight tube but you need to know where your heel will fall, so, again accurate measurements are needed.

Knit the length of foot or leg that you think will suffice; for the foot this is approximately 2in short of your actual foot length, then half way across the tube drop your main yarn and knit the next half of your total number of stitches with a length of waste yarn. Return the stitches to the right needle, pick up your main yarn again and knit over those same stitches, then continue knitting in the round until the tube is finished all but the toe. Shape the toe as you would normally, noting which method you have used as you can use the same one for the heel.

Using a needle one or two sizes smaller than you are working with, slip it through the stitches that were worked in the waste yarn. If you are using a circular needle, next, turn the sock upside down and slip the needle through the stitches below the waste yarn. Carefully tease out the waste yarn. Change to your working needle and complete the heel as for the toe. If you are using double pointed needles use one for the top stitches and a second one for the lower ones, then arrange the stitches evenly over three or four needles. Unless you have worked a wedge shaped toe and heel where you need to graft the remaining stitches together, the sock is now virtually finished and just needs the ends darning in.

If the sock is worked toe up you will need to work out where the heel needs to be placed. It should come between two and three inches short of the total length of the foot from the toe to the back of the heel. A cardboard template made of your foot is useful for several techniques but especially for this one. If the start of the heel is marked on this template the heel will be a better fit than if you make a rough guess.

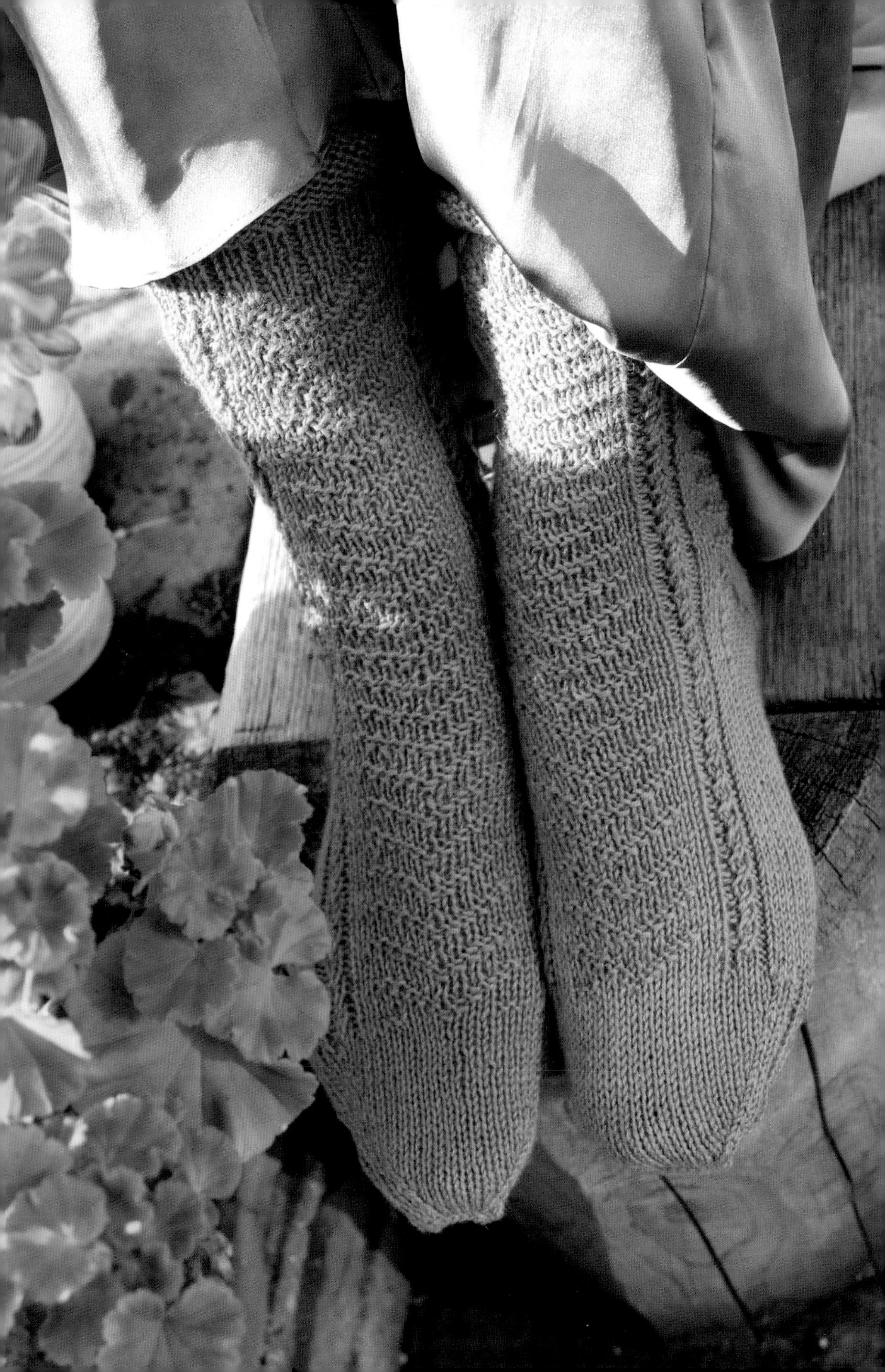

CHAPTER 4

Toes

Most socks are worked beginning at the cuff and working downwards, shaping the heel and then knitting the foot until it is approximately 2 inches shorter than the required length. This measurement is for the toe, which is shaped in various ways and often necessitates joining stitches together at the finish either by casting the stitches off together on the wrong side, or by grafting them closed using Kitchener stitch. The different ways of shaping the toes are described here and any of the patterns in the book can make use of the different toe shapings according to preference.

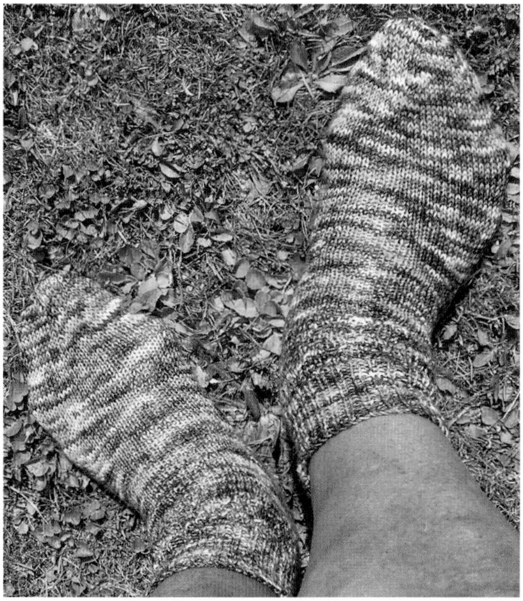

The Three Point Toe on the Phoenix socks.

Before you choose which method to use for shaping the toe, make a diagram of your own foot. Place your foot on a piece of card and draw around your toes. Look at the shape. Is it pointed, straight across, rounded, is your big toe extra long? All of these factors will determine which type of toe shaping will fit best and whether you need to decrease/increase more or less frequently than described in the instructions. The diagram will also help you to decide where to start shaping after working the foot. Most patterns are based on an average toe length of 2–2½ inches, but the sock will be more comfortable if you can make the foot long enough that the tip of the big toe will fit the sock exactly.

TIP

Standing on a piece of graph paper to draw around your foot will give you an even more accurate idea of when and where to make the shapings. This is especially helpful if you are working the anatomically correct shape with a different left and right foot.

SOCKS WORKED FROM THE CUFF DOWN

Wedge toe

This was the most common way of working the toe of a sock and gives a triangular shape that needs finishing off with grafting or casting the stitches off together. Grafting gives a toe without a ridge of stitches on the inside that can rub. If you don't like, or haven't mastered grafting, casting the stitches off together on the right side will cause less friction.

1. When the foot is long enough (usually approximately 5cm/2in less than the foot measurement), divide the stitches in half and place a marker at each of the half-way points.
2. *Knit to 3 stitches before the marker, k2tog, k2, ssk; repeat from * for the second half of stitches. Knit 1 round.
3. Repeat the last 2 rounds until there are approximately one third of the original stitches left on the needles. Graft or cast off these stitches together.

Rounded toe

1. Divide the toe evenly into eight sections. If necessary, place markers at each section to make it easier to see where to make the decreases.
2. Knit to 2 stitches before each marker, k2tog.
3. Work 1 or more rounds, depending on the shape of the toes.
4. Repeat these 2 steps until half of the stitches are used, then continue working the decreases on every round to approximately 8 stitches.
5. Thread the yarn through the remaining stitches, draw up firmly and fasten off.
6. To give a more rounded toe, work 5 rounds after the first decrease round, 3 rounds after the next 2 decrease rounds and 1 round after each of the next decrease rounds.

Asymmetrical toe

The decreases can also be worked on one side only for the first few times to accommodate a long big toe. Then work them at both ends and complete as for the wedge toe. The Bullfinch sock in Chapter 5 has asymmetric toes.

JOINING THE FINAL FEW STITCHES TO FINISH THE TOE

For all of these cuff down socks there will be a few stitches left at the end of the toe. To avoid a hard ridge at this point, graft the stitches together (known as Kitchener stitch). If you find this difficult, use a three-needle cast off.

Three needle cast off

1. Turn the socks inside out.
2. With right sides together and with the same number of stitches on each needle, take a third needle and knit together both of the first stitches on each needle.
3. Knit the next two stitches on each needle together.
4. Cast off knitwise over both pairs of stitches.
5. Continue in this way, casting off pairs of stitches to the end.

Kitchener stitch (grafting)

1. Cut off the yarn leaving enough to thread backwards and forwards through all of the stitches left on the needles.
2. With wrong sides together and the same number of stitches on each needle take a large-eyed, blunt-tip needle (tapestry needle) and thread the cut end through the eye of the needle.
3. Take the tapestry needle through the first stitch on the front knitting needle purlwise, leaving the stitch on the knitting needle.
4. Take the tapestry needle through the first stitch on the back needle knitwise, and leave the stitch on the knitting needle.
5. Take the tapestry needle through the first stitch on the front needle knitwise, and slip the stitch off the knitting needle.
6. Take the tapestry needle through the next stitch on the front needle purlwise, and leave it on the knitting needle.

7. Take the tapestry needle through the stitch on the back needle purlwise, and slip the stitch off the knitting needle.
8. Take the tapestry needle through the next stitch on the back needle knitwise, and leave it on the needle.
9. Repeat the last 4 steps until there is one stitch left. Take the tail end through that stitch and weave it firmly into the knitting.

The stitches should all be grafted through so that they appear to be at the same tension as the knitting.

TIP

A form of Kitchener stitch can also be used to create a very stretchy top edge by sewing through the last row of stitches of a cuff alternately purlwise and knitwise.

TOES THAT DON'T REQUIRE GRAFTING

Hat top

This makes a rounded shape and is worked in the same way as the crown of a knitted hat or beanie. It is best worked over an even number of stitches that will divide exactly. It is finished off by taking the yarn through the last remaining stitches, drawing it up firmly and fastening off into the inside of the sock.

An example for a foot with 64 stitches

1. (k6, k2tog) to end of round. Eight stitches have been decreased and will be each time.
2. Work 3 or 4 rounds and then decrease again as follows: (k5, k2tog). Continue in this way, working 1 less stitch between each decrease and 1 or 2 rounds without decreasing until the round (k1, k2tog) has been completed.
3. k2tog all across the last round.
4. Thread the yarn through the remaining stitches and pull it tight to close the hole. Thread it through again to make it firm and fasten off the end of yarn on the inside.

Star toe

This toe shape is slightly conical and more pointed than a rounded hat toe.

1. Begin by dividing the stitches into four equal sections and place a marker at each division. At each section, knit to 2 stitches before the marker and k2tog.
2. Knit the next round(s). For a longer toe shape, work 2 or 3 rounds before each round of decreasing until the last 3 rounds, then work decreases on alternate rounds.
3. Repeat these rounds until there are about 8 stitches left.
4. Thread yarn through, draw up firmly and fasten off.

In all of these shapings the frequency of the decreases determines the length of the toe and the sharpness of the angle.

These different ways of shaping can also be used for toe up socks, increasing in the appropriate places instead of decreasing. But there are other ways of shaping the toes of socks worked from the toe up and the neatest way is to create a rounded shape by working short rows.

STARTING AT THE TOE

Flat cast on

Instead of casting on all the stitches at once, a neat toe can be made by casting on half of the stitches, knitting two rows and then picking up the same number of stitches from the other side before joining them into a circle. Make the increases at the side edges as for a wedge toe or space them evenly for a more rounded toe.

Crochet cast on for starting a circle

Using a circular or dpns, knit those loops one by one onto the needle, being careful to keep the stitches in the correct order, knit 1 round.

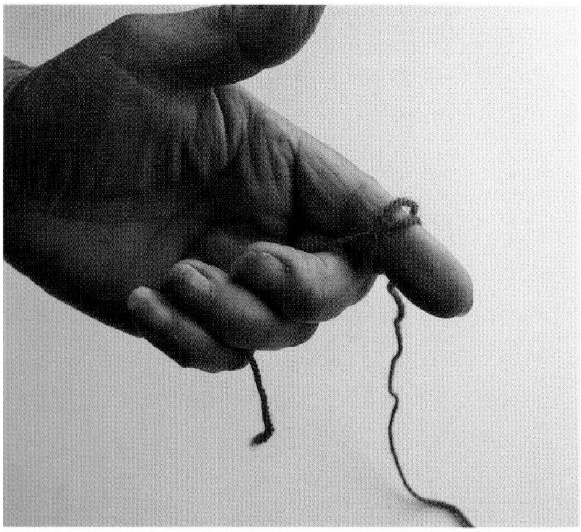

Step 1: Make a loop in the yarn, leaving a tail about 6 inches long.

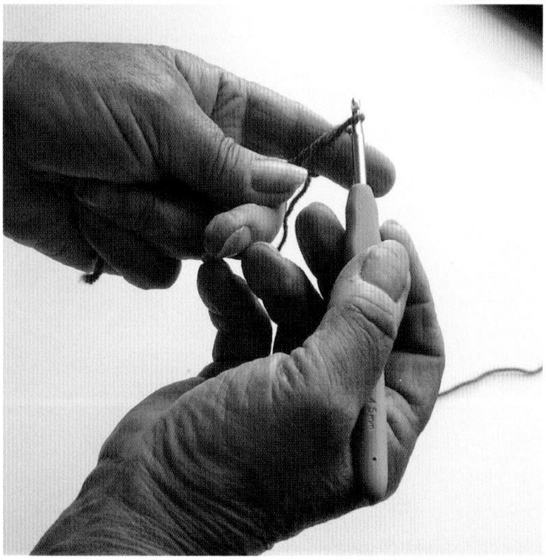

Step 3: Wrap the yarn around the hook and pull it through the loop on the hook. Repeat steps 2 and 3 until you have the desired number of stitches.

Circular cast on without a crochet hook

1. Make a circle of yarn around one or two fingers.
2. Insert the point of a needle into the centre of the loop, back behind the working yarn,

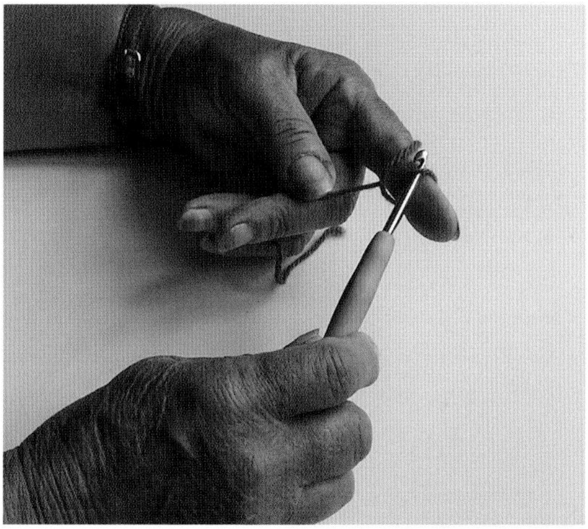

Step 2: With a crochet hook the same size or one size larger than the needles used for the sock, pull a strand of working yarn through the loop.

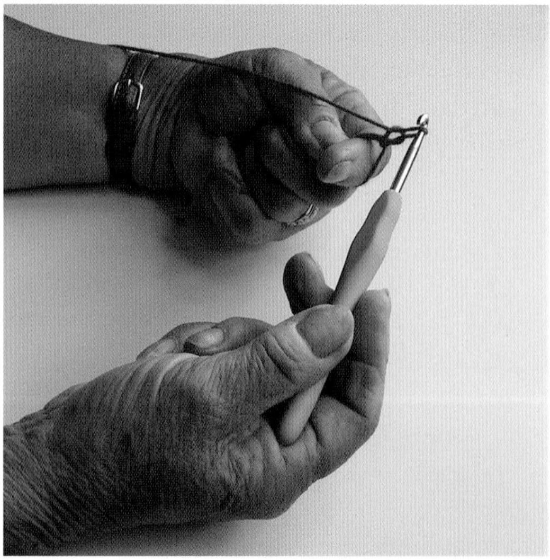

Step 4: Pull on the tail end to close the loop.

catching the strand and bringing it forwards through the loop onto the needle.

3. Keeping the fingers within the loop, make a yarn over.
4. Repeat steps 2 and 3 for the number of stitches required.

The following rounds will require gradual increases to shape the toe and reach the correct number of stitches for the foot.

TIP

Thread the yarn through the loops several times to make a firm closure. The hole can have a tendency to come open during wear if it is not fastened off tightly enough.

Turkish cast on

This is easiest to work on a circular needle as you can slide the bottom half of the stitches onto the cable before knitting those on the top needle tip.

1. Make a slip knot on one needle.
2. Hold two double-pointed needles with both tips pointing right.
3. Wrap the working yarn from front to back around both needles for the required number of stitches, not counting the slip knot.
4. Carefully knit the stitches on the top needle.
5. Turn and knit the stitches from the other needle.

Judy's magic cast on

This method is best used when working with a circular needle. It was discovered, perhaps invented, by Judy Becker who didn't like the loose-looking stitches at the toe when using other methods. It is written as though the circular needle were two separate needles to make it easier to describe.

Continue repeating steps 3 and 4, alternating between needle one and needle two until you have cast on the desired number of stitches with the same number on each needle tip.

The top strand on the index finger always wraps around needle one (the bottom needle), and the bottom strand from the thumb always wraps around needle two (the top needle).

To begin knitting

1. Remove the slip knot and drop the yarn tail. Turn the needles so that needle 1 is on the top.
2. Slide the stitches on needle 2 to the right so that the stitches lie on the cable.
3. Knit the row of stitches from needle 1. The first stitch will probably look loose so pull gently on the tail to tighten it back up. A row of stitches will appear between the two needles.

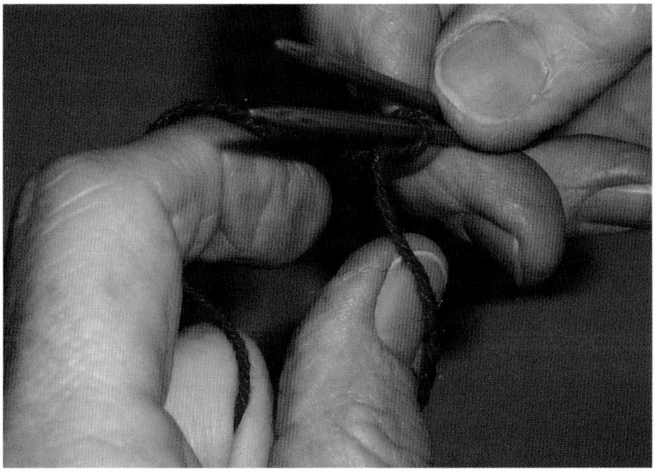

Step 1: Make a slip knot with a long tail and place it on one of the needles.

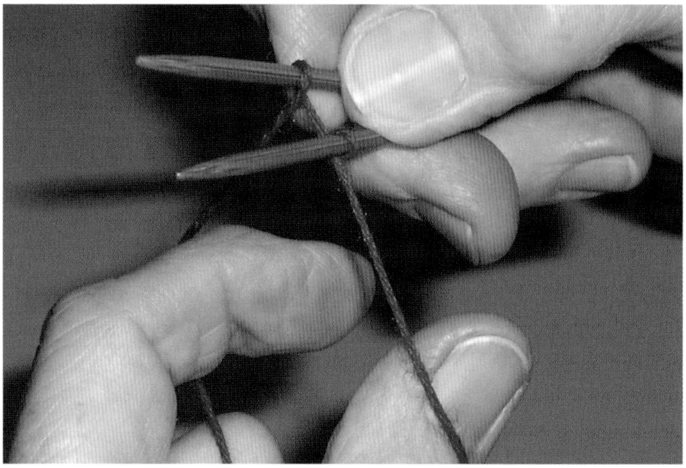

Step 2: Hold the two ends of the needle together pointing to the left and with the needle tip that has the slip knot toward the top. This is needle two. Hold the yarn with the tail over your index finger and the working yarn over your thumb.
Step 3: Bring the tip of the lower needle (needle one) over the strand of yarn on your finger.

Step 4: Take the yarnbetween the two needles,and back up, making a loop around needle. Pull the loop snug, but not tight, around the needle making a stitch on needle one.

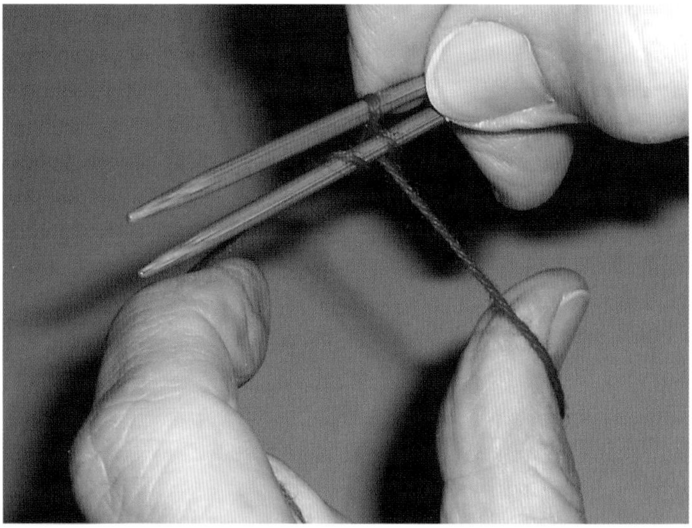

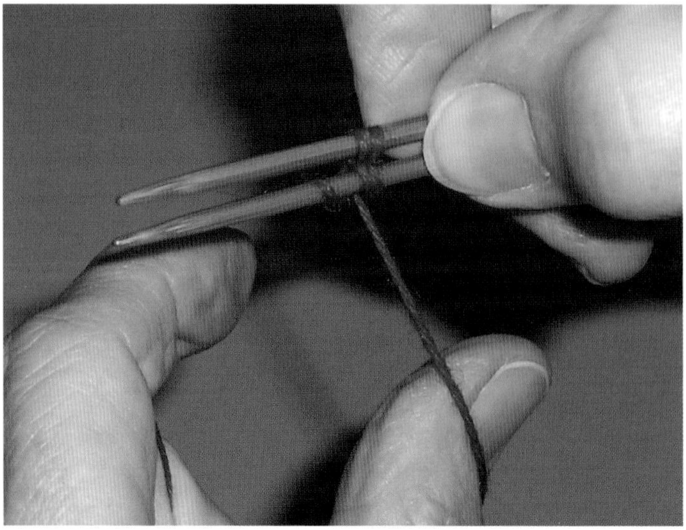

Step 5: Bring needle two over the yarn tail on your thumb, around and under the yarn and back up, making a loop around needle two. Pull the loop snug around the needle making a stitch on needle two.

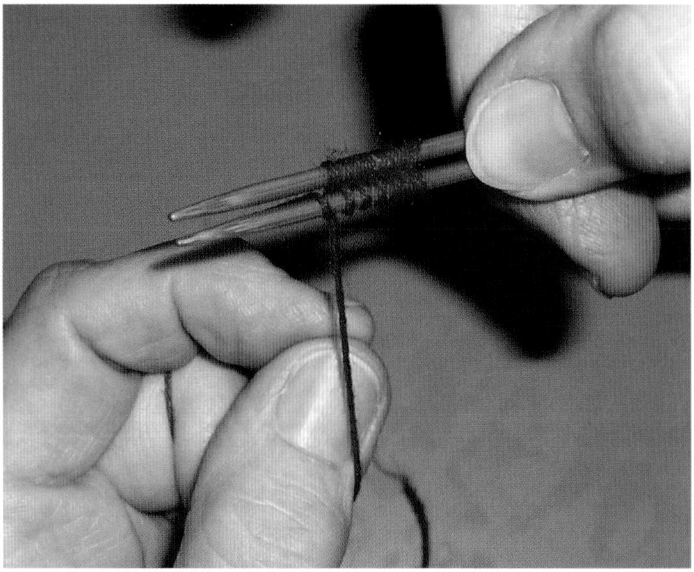

Step 6: Repeat step 3 to cast a second stitch on to needle one. (Bottom around top).

Step 7: Repeat step 4 to cast a second stitch on to needle two. The slip knot does not count as a stitch and will be removed.

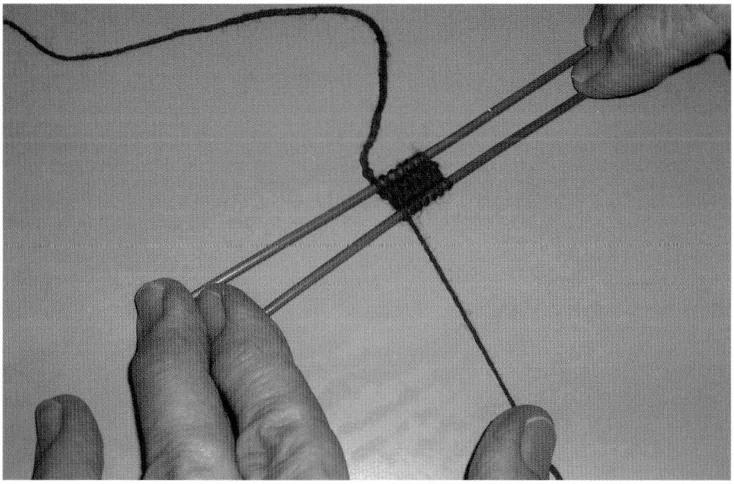

4. Slide the stitches from needle 1 onto the cable.
5. Arrange needle 2 so that its point is towards the right and knit the stitches from it.

Note: The cast-on loops on needle 2 will be twisted so on the first round knit them through the back of the loops in order to untwist them. After this round the stitches will be aligned as normal.

There are now two rows of stitches between the needles and you can continue to work in the round, increasing as instructed for the start of the foot.

INCREASING FOR TOE UP SOCKS

Working a sock from the toe up has the advantage of making it easy to adjust the fit by trying it on as you knit. This is naturally easier when working on a long circular needle, but it can be done carefully with a set of dpns. Another advantage is that the length of leg is easy to adjust if there is only a limited amount of yarn.

A disadvantage is that casting on to begin the closed toe can be a bit awkward at first. After the initial cast-on row, it is necessary to increase to the required number of stitches for the foot and the rest of the sock. There are different ways of doing this and all of the toes that are shaped by decreasing as for cuff down socks can be worked in a similar way by increasing at that position, either invisibly or by lifting the horizontal thread between the stitches and knitting into the back of it.

For example: cast on 8 stitches and join them into a round. If you are using two circulars or a set of dpns divide them equally to make it easier to see where to place the increases. Place four on each of two circular needles or two on each of four dpns, for example. Knit one round on these eight stitches, then increase in every stitch. Knit another round then increase in every alternate stitch. Knit a further round then increase in every third stitch; continue in this way, working one more stitch between the increases until there are the required number of stitches.

Rounded toe

1. Cast on one third of the required number of stitches for the foot and knit one round.
2. Divide the work into three sections and place a marker at each division.
3. *K1, m1, k to 2 stitches before marker, m1, k1. Repeat from * to end of round.
4. Knit next round.
5. Repeat these 2 rounds until there are the required number of stitches for the foot.

Wedge toe

1. Cast on 12 stitches and place markers at the beginning of the round and after 6 stitches.
2. *K1, m1L, k4, m1R, k1; repeat from * to the second marker and repeat from * for the next half of stitches. Knit 1 round.
3. Repeat the last 2 rounds until there are the required number of stitches for the foot.

Once the toe and foot are completed it is time to turn the heel.

SHORT ROW SHAPING FOR THE HEELS OF TOE UP SOCKS

After working the toes and the correct length of foot as per the template, work 2 rows then start the short row shaping.

Wrap and turn

This is the basic method that most knitters seem familiar with. Leaving one stitch unworked on each row then working back over each stitch one at a time, making a further wrap and turn, will create a smooth rounded toe. The method is described in detail on page 36.

When all the wrapped stitches have been worked, continue knitting in the round for the rest of the foot. Work a short row heel to match the toe then continue to knit for the required length of the leg.

Simple short rows

This method can leave small holes if you don't tighten the yarn enough, but it is the easiest way of working short rows for toes or heels. There is no wrapping or picking up wraps on the return rows.

1. Knit as far as the last stitch; turn.
2. Slip the next stitch purlwise and pull on the yarn to tighten it, purl the next stitch and tighten that too; turn.
3. Work to the last stitch before the slipped one of the next row and repeat the slipping, tightening, working the next stitch and tightening that too. When working back over the stitches, tighten the slipped ones again and this should avoid a hole.

German short rows

1. Work to the turning point.
2. Slip the next stitch purlwise from the left needle to the right.

3. Tug the working yarn so that it goes over the top of the needle making two legs of the stitch lie on the needle.
4. Repeat these 2 steps for the required number of stitches, then on the return rows, work through the two legs together as if they were one stitch.

Fleegle heel

This heel is worked on toe up socks where the gusset is created first. It is an alternative to a short row heel. Stitches are increased each side of the instep and then decreased for the second part of the heel. The method is used on the Serin socks in Chapter 5.

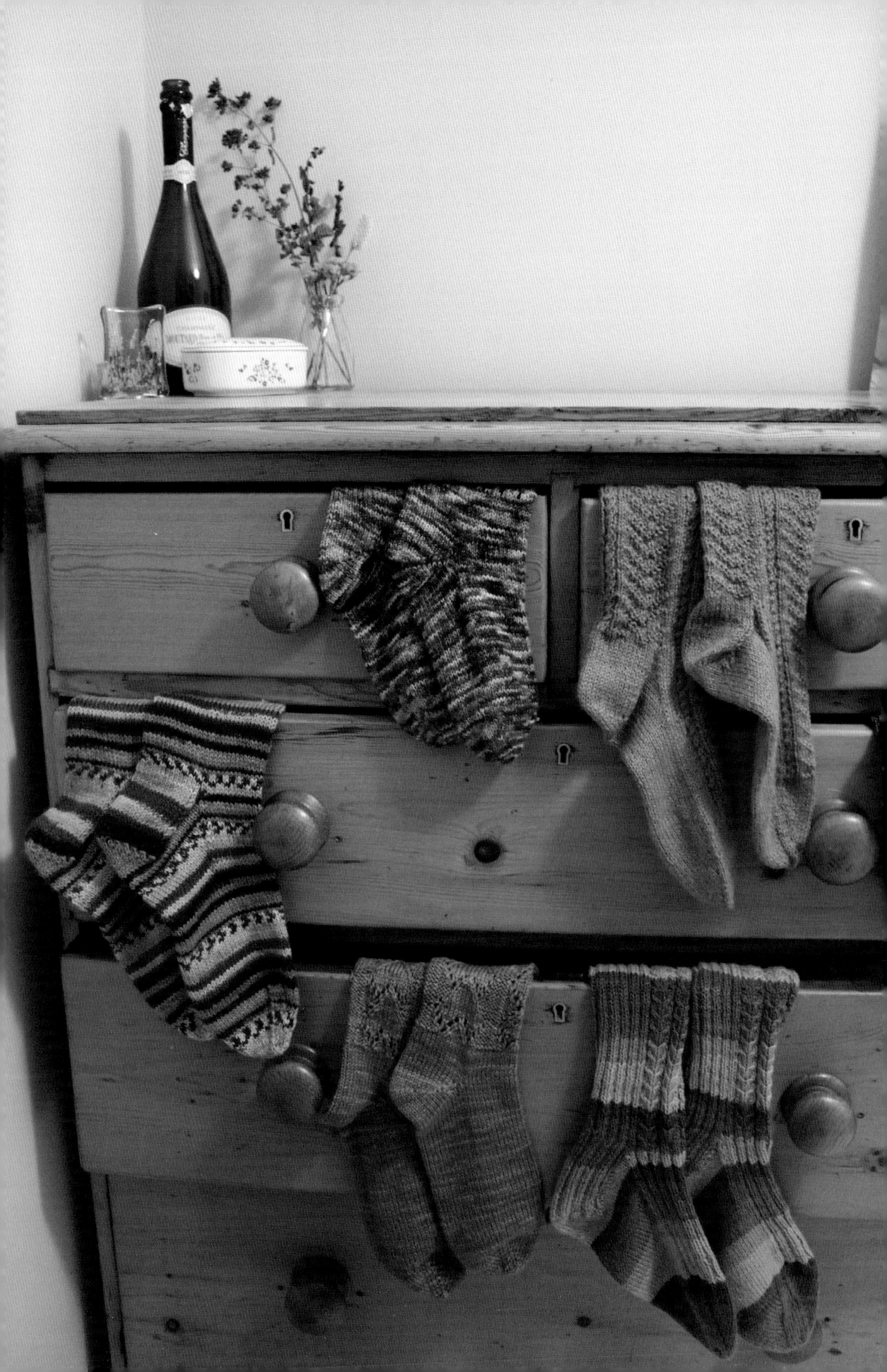

CHAPTER 5

The Projects

ARCTIC TERN

These socks are mid-calf length but, like most of the patterns, the length of leg and foot can be made to fit any size. The socks are ribbed to grip the leg but they also feature four simple cables running down the front of the leg, growing on from the knit 2 purl 2 rib. They are worked from the top down with a ribbed heel flap, rounded heel and a wedge toe.

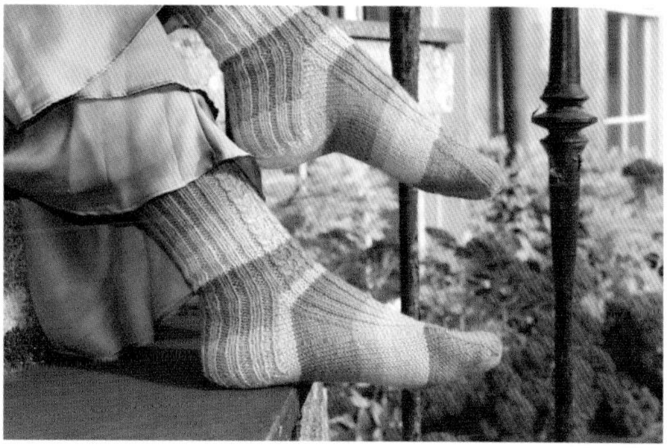

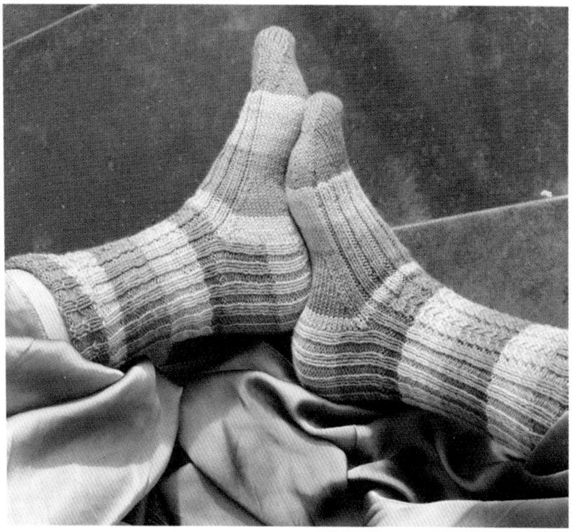

Materials: 300g 4-ply (West Yorkshire Spinners); 3.00mm needles.
Size: circumference of foot 24cm/9½in; length of leg 22cm/8½in; length of foot 24cm/9½in.
Tension: 30sts and 38 rounds to 10cm/4in on 3.00mm needles over st st.

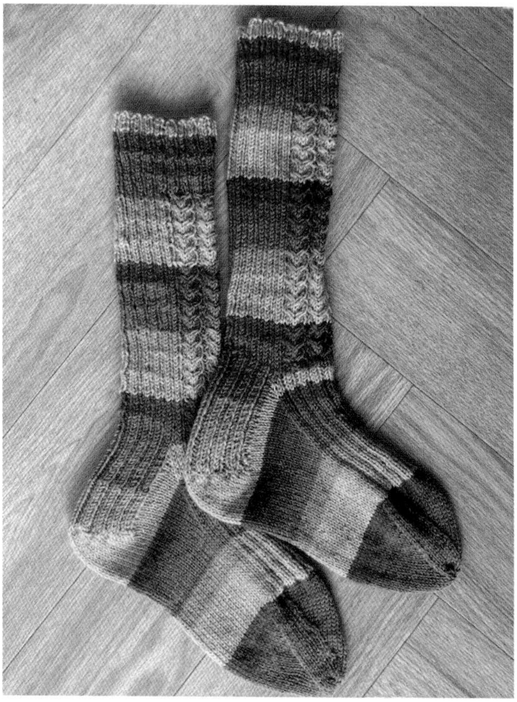

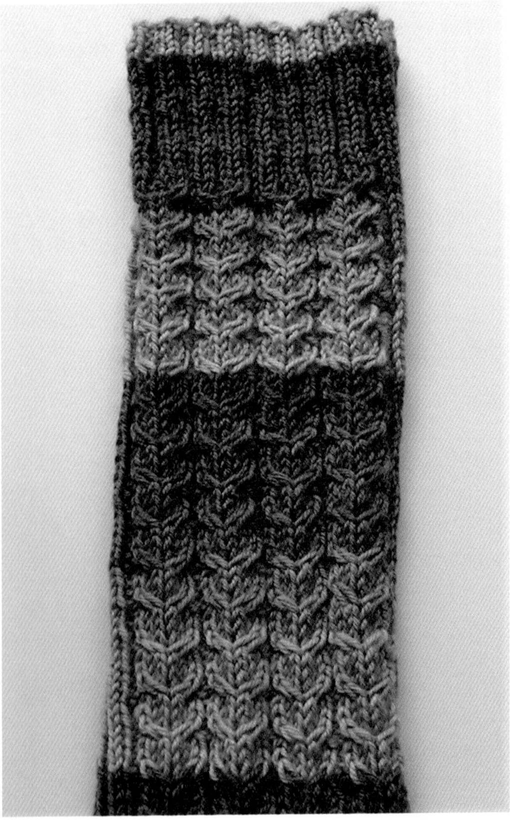

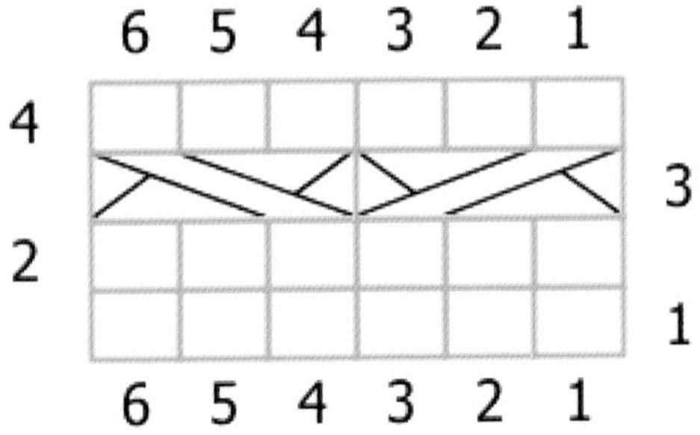

Arctic Tern chart.

Cable pattern

Row 1 (RS): knit. (6sts)
Row 2 (WS): purl.
Row 3: 1/2 RC: slip next 2 stitches to cable needle and place at back of work, k1, then k2 from cable needle; 1/2 LC: slip next stitch to cable needle and place at front of work, k2, then k1 from cable needle.
Row 4: purl.

Instructions

Make two socks the same.

Cast on 72sts, divide sts over 3 needles and join into a ring, being careful not to twist.

Work in rib for 24 rounds as follows: k1 (p2, k2) to last 3, p2, k1.

If necessary, re-arrange the sts on the needles to make it easier to work the cables but place a marker at the beginning of the rounds.

Next round: work 23sts in rib as set (Gullwing, p2) 3 times, Gullwing, rib to end.
Work in pattern as set for 20cm/8in.

Start heel

Rib 18, slip last 18 of round onto other end of same needle (36sts for heel flap).

Leave rem 36sts on 2 needles for instep.

Work 30 rows rib on 36sts, slipping first st of every row and ending on a purl row.

Turn heel

Next round: k22, k2tog, turn.
Next round: sl1, p8, p2tog, turn.
Next round: sl1, k9, k2tog, turn.
Next round: sl1, p10, p2tog, turn.

Continue in this way until there are 22sts on needle.

Next round: 1st needle: k22, pick up and knit 17 along side of heel; 2nd needle: rib 36;
3rd needle: pick up and knit 17 along other side of heel, k11. This point marks the start of the rounds.
Work 1 round as set.
Next round: 1st needle: k to last 3sts, k2tog, k1; 2nd needle: rib; 3rd needle, k1, ssk, k to end.

Repeat these 2 rounds until there are 72sts.

Continue working foot as set to 20cm/8in, or length required.

Shape toe

Decreasing on every alt round as follows:
1st needle: k to last 4sts, k2tog, k2.
2nd needle: k2, ssk, k to last 4sts, k2tog, k2
3rd needle: k2 ssk, k to end.
When there are 28sts altogether, graft or cast them off together on the inside.

Finishing

Darn in any ends. Block and press.

BULLFINCH

This sock starts from the cuff and has a simple cable pattern on the leg, twisting in opposite directions depending on which leg it is for. The heel flap is ribbed and the heel itself is a square, Dutch heel. The foot and toe are plain stocking stitch but the toe is unusual in that it is asymmetrical to accommodate a long big toe.

Materials: 100g [150, 200, 250] 4-ply sock wool. These were knitted using Skein Queen Crush sock wool in shade Royal Ascot. 2.25mm and 2.75mm needles.
Foot size: 18.5cm [23.5]/7½in [9½].
Tension: 32sts and 40 rows to 10cm over st st using 2.75mm needles.

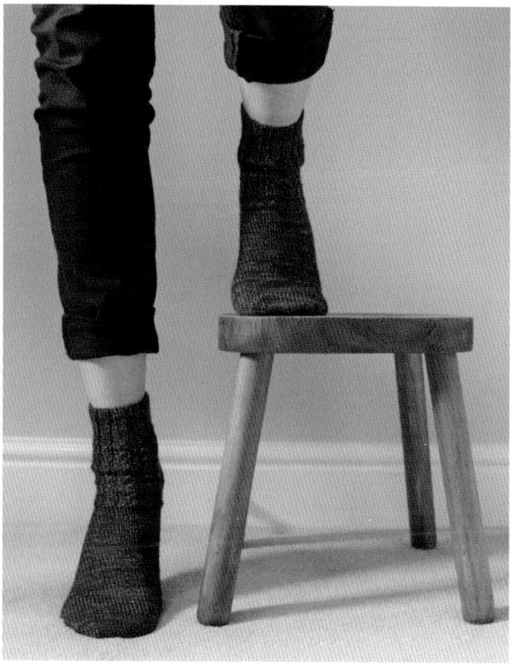

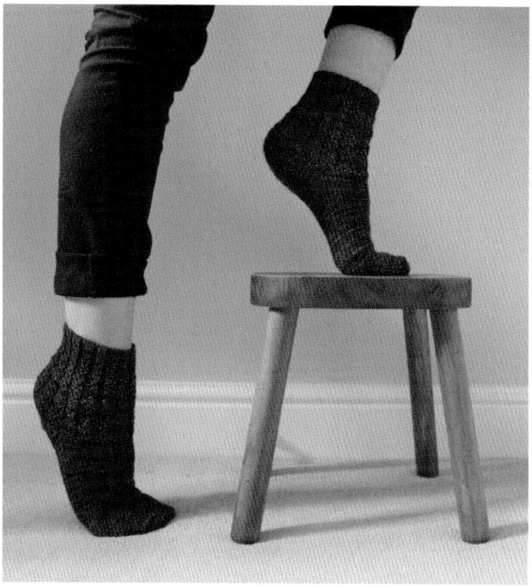

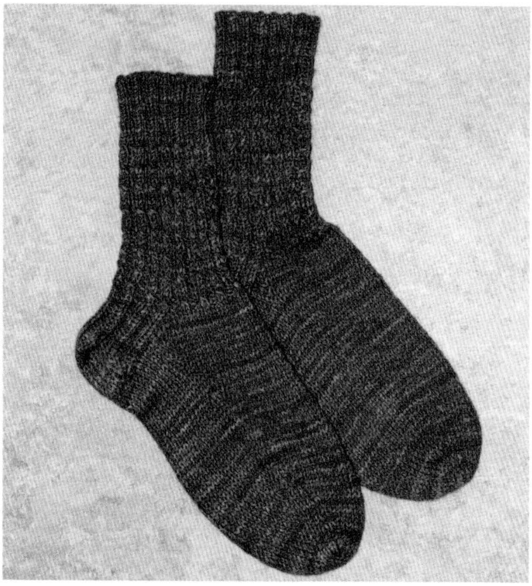

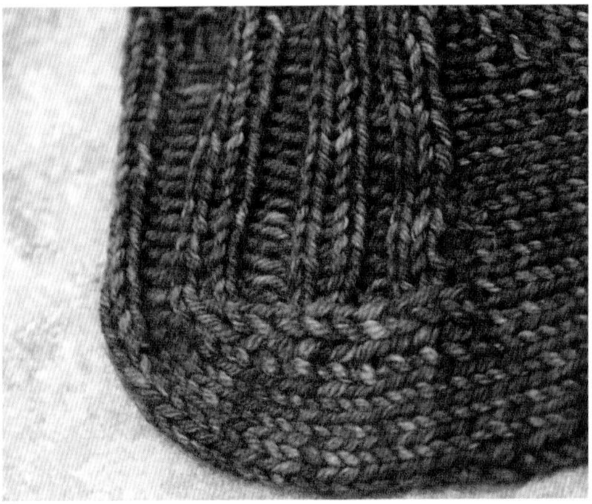

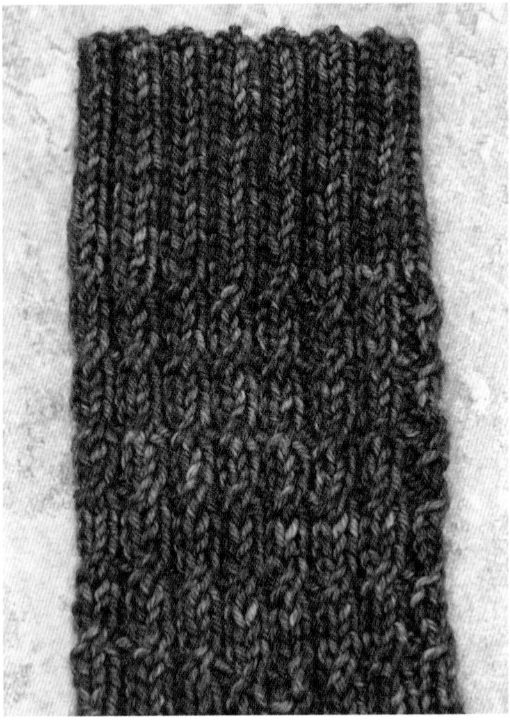

Cable pattern for right sock

Round 1: p2, k2.
Round 2: p2, tw2L.
Rounds 3, 4 & 5: as for round 1.

Cable pattern for left sock

Round 1: p2, k2.
Round 2: p2, tw2R.
Rounds 3, 4 & 5: as for round 1.

Instructions

Using 2.75mm needles, cast on 60 [72] sts and join to work in the round.
Change to 2.25mm needles and work 18 rounds of p2, k2 rib.
Change to 2.75mm needles and cont in cable rib, twisting the stitches to the right or left depending on which sock you are working.
When leg measures 18cm/7in work on one set of sts as follows, leaving rem sts on spare needles.

Shape heel

Rib 15 [18], slip next 5 (9) to following needle, turn.
sl1, rib 29 [35] as set.

Cont on these 30 [36] sts for 7.5cm/3in.

Turn heel

Row 1: sl1, k19 [23], ssk, turn.
Row 2: sl1, p10 [12], p2tog, turn.
Row 3: sl1, k10 [12] ssk, turn.

Cont in this way until all sts have been worked. Sl1, k to end.

Cont in st st on 60 [72] sts until foot is required length less 6cm/2½in for toe.

Shape toe

Left sock

Starting at beginning of round, i.e. centre of heel.
Next round: k12 [15], k2tog, k2, ssk, k to end.
Work 2 rounds without shaping.
Next round: k11 [14], k2tog, k2, ssk, k to end.
Work 2 rounds without shaping.

Cont decreasing every 3rd round to 54 [56] sts then every alt round to 44 [46] sts

Now dec at both sides of toe on alt rounds to 20 [22] sts.

Graft or cast off sts together.

Right sock

K43 [51], k2tog, k2, ssk, k to end.

Cont as for left sock, reversing shaping.

Graft or cast off sts together.

Finishing

Darn in any ends. Block and press.

HERRING GULL

These socks are worked top down and feature a traditional gansey herringbone pattern around the leg and on the instep. They have a standard heel flap with a V turn and gusset shaping in keeping with the style of a fisherman's gansey. The toe has stitches cast off together on the right side to resemble the shoulder strap of a gansey.

Materials: 100g West Yorkshire Spinners Signature 4-ply (75 per cent wool, 25 per cent nylon), 400m/437yds. 2.75mm needles.
Sizes: to fit small [large].
Tension: 28sts and 36 rows to 10cm/4in on 3.00mm needles over pattern.

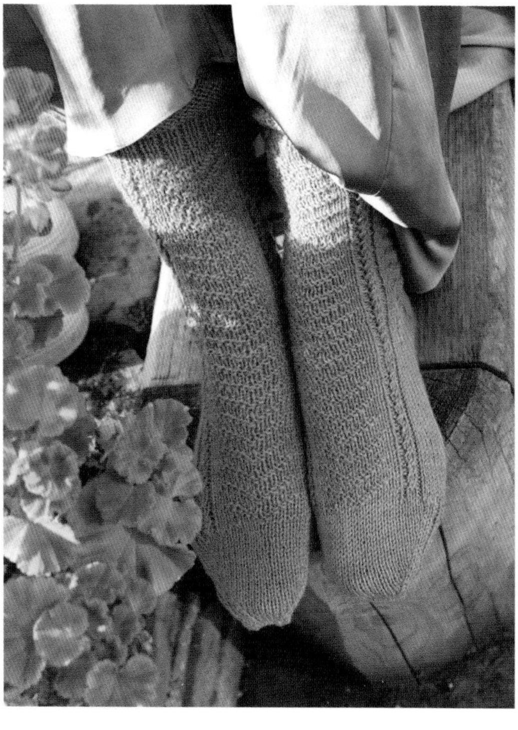

Instructions

Make two socks the same.

Cast on 57 [63] sts.

Work 3cm/1¼in in garter st then 9 rounds k2 p1 rib.

Now work from chart or written instructions until leg measures 18cm/7in or length required, working stitches marked in red and green for large size only.

Textured pattern

Round 1: p1, k2, p1, k17. (21sts)
Round 2: p1, 1/1 RC, p1, k3, p2, k7, p2, k3.
Round 3: p1, k2, p1, k4, p2, k5, p2, k4.
Round 4: p1, k2, p1, k5, p2, k3, p2, k5.
Round 5: p1, 1/1 RC, p1, k6, p2, k1, p2, k6.
Round 6: p1, k2, p1, k7, p3, k7.
Round 7: p1, k2, (p1, k3, p2, k3) × 2.

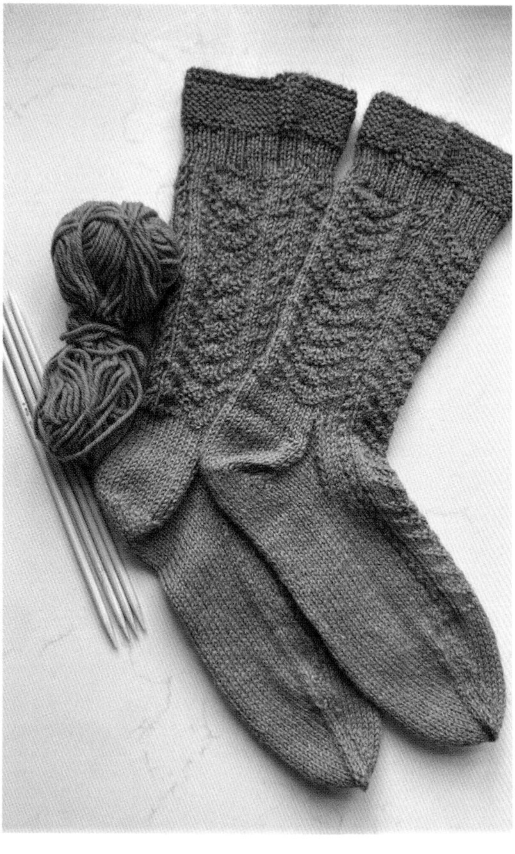

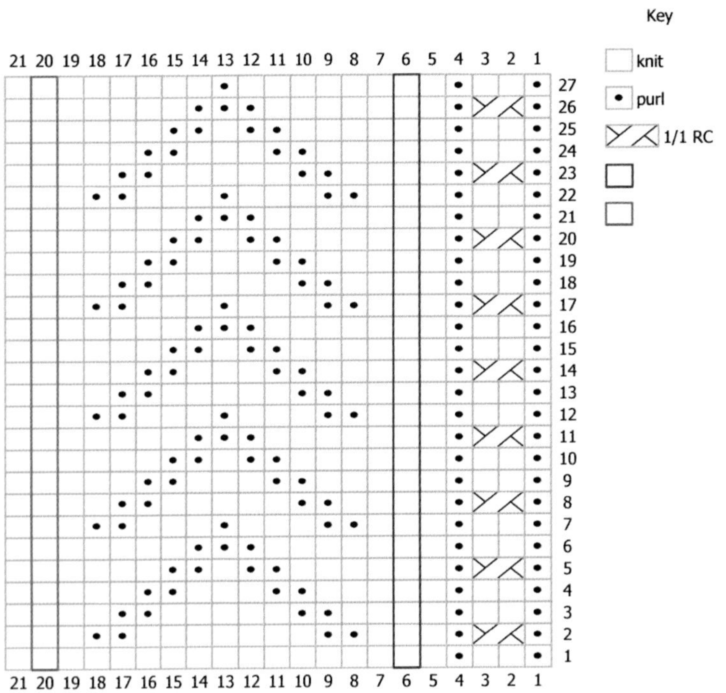

Herringbone chart.

Round 8: p1, 1/1 RC, p1, k4, p2, k5, p2, k4.

Continue following placement of cables and herringbones until leg is required length.

Shape heel

Knit 5, work 19 [21] sts in pattern as on chart, knit 5, knit 28 [30] sts for heel.

Work approx. 2in in st st, slipping the first st of every row and ending with WS facing.

Turn heel

Row 1: sl1, p16 (17), p2tog, p1, turn.
Row 2: sl1, k5, ssk, k1, turn.
Row 3: sl1, p6, ptog, p1, turn.
Row 4: sl1, k7, ssk, k1, turn.

Cont in this way adding one more st each time until all sts are used and RS is facing.

Knit across all sts.

Gusset

Pick up and knit into every slipped stitch alongside of heel flap.

To avoid what sometimes forms a hole here, pick up the horizontal bar before the next stitch and knit into the back of it, pm.

Work in pattern across instep sts, pick up the horizontal bar before the next stitch and knit into the back of it, pm.

Pick up and knit into every slipped stitch along other side of heel.

Knit 1 round.

K to 2sts before 1st marker, k2tog: k until 2nd marker is passed, ssk, k to end of round.

Knit 1 round without shaping.

Repeat these 2 rounds until sts are reduced to 55 [63]. Remove markers.

Cont in st st for sole and following chart for top of foot, placing 4 stitch cable panel at each side of herringbone panel. When foot is required length minus approx. 6cm/2½in for toe, increase one stitch at centre back. 56 [64] sts.

Shape toe

Working in st st with purl 'seam' stitches decrease as follows:

Round 1: p1, k27 [31], p1, k to end
Round 2: *p1, k1, ssk, k to 3sts before next p stitch, k2tog, k1; repeat from * to end.

Work 2 rounds without shaping

Repeat these 4 rounds twice more, then rounds 1 and 2 until there are 10sts left.

Cast off these sts together on the right side.

Finishing

Darn in all ends. Block and press.

JAY

A basic sock with a French heel and grafted wedge toe. It is made interesting by the use of a yarn that is dyed in such a way that it creates a pattern as you knit. The yarn is described as DK but working it on smaller needles than suggested gives a firm fabric for a hardwearing sock.

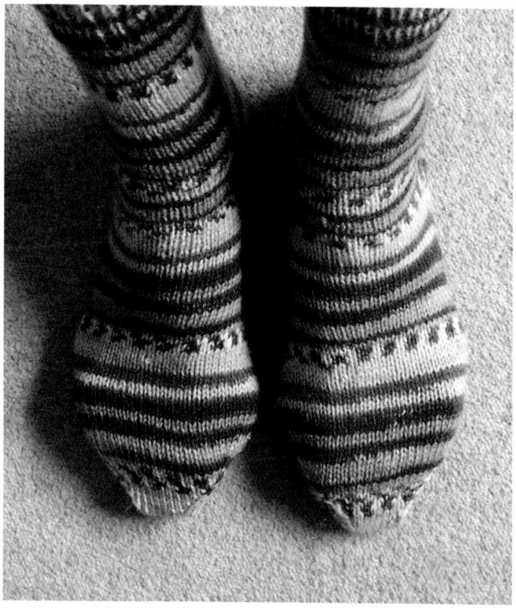

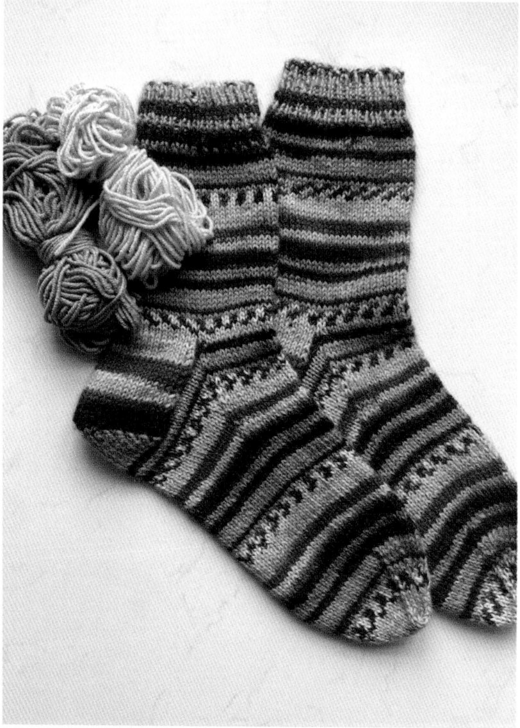

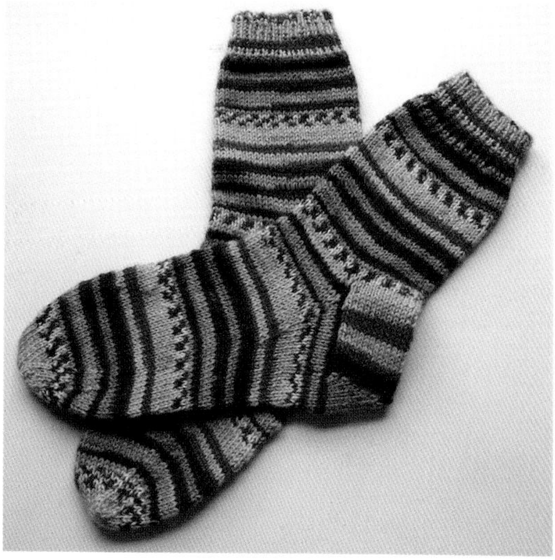

Materials: 100g [100, 150, 150] sock wool. These were knitted using Adriafil.
Knitcol shade no 73. Needles: set of 4 dpns size 2.75mm.
Foot circumference: 15cm [18.5, 23.5, 27]/6in [7½, 9½, 10½].
Tension: 30sts and 40 rows to 10cm over st st using 2.75mm needles.

Instructions

Make two socks the same.

Using 2.75mm needles, cast on 48 [56, 64, 72] sts and join to work in the round.

Work in k1 p1 rib for 12 rounds.

Change to st st for leg and cont until work measures 17cm/7in or length required.

Start heel

Knit 24 [28, 32, 36] sts and leave remainder for instep.

Work 6cm/2½in in st st, slipping the first stitch of each row and ending with WS facing.

Turn heel

Row 1: sl1, p16 [18, 20, 22], p2tog, p1, turn.
Row 2: sl1, k3, ssk, k1, turn.
Row 3: sl1, p4, p2tog, p1, turn.
Row 4: sl1, k5, ssk, k1, turn.

Cont in this way until all sts have been worked ending with RS facing. Knit one row on all heel sts if necessary.

Gusset

Pick up and knit 1 stitch for each of the slipped sts alongside of heel flap, 24 [28, 32, 36] sts from those left on holder, pick up and knit 1 for each of the slipped sts along other side of heel flap, then knit 12 [14, 16, 18] from heel. The next stitch will be the start of the round.

Work 1 round, placing markers before and after the 24 [28, 32, 36] sts of the instep.

Next round: knit to 2sts before 1st marker, k2tog; knit to 2nd marker, ssk, k to end of round.
Next round: knit.
Repeat these 2 rounds until there are 48 [56, 64, 72] sts.

Cont in rounds without shaping until foot is required length less 6cm/2½in for toe.

Arrange sts so that there are 12 [14,16,18] on 1st needle, 24 [28, 32, 36] on 2nd and 12 [14,16,18] on 3rd.

Shape toe

Next round: k to 3sts before end of 1st needle, k2tog, k1; k1, ssk, k to last 3 on 2nd needle, k2tog, k1; k1, ssk, k to end of round.
K2 rounds.
Repeat dec round.
K2 rounds.
Repeat dec round.
K1 round.
Repeat dec round.
Repeat last 2 rounds until there are 12sts left.
Graft or cast off these sts together on the inside.

Finishing

Darn in any ends and block socks as described on page 17.

LINNET

A basic sock made a little out of the ordinary by the addition of an optional lacy cuff. These were knitted using a variegated yarn but they could be worked in a plain yarn to highlight the lace pattern. It is a useful pattern that comes in several sizes to amend and adapt as you please. The socks have a French heel and a hat toe, which means there is no grafting to do!

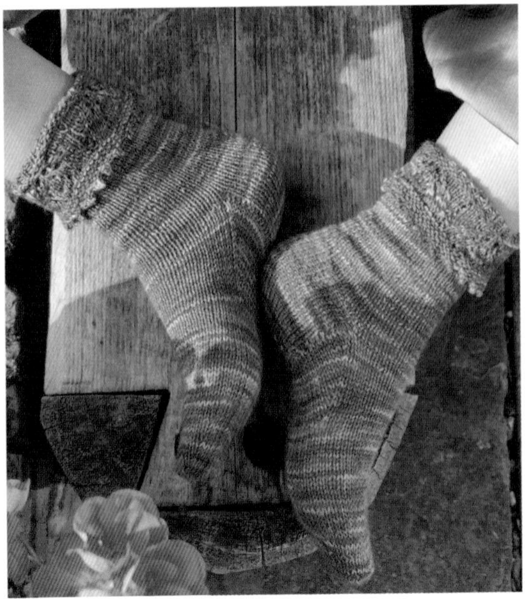

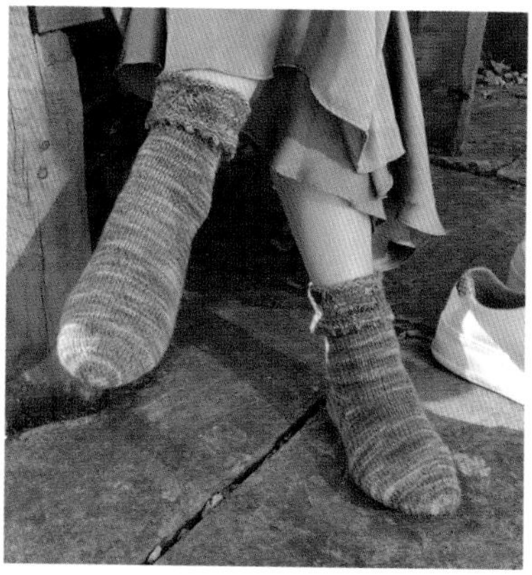

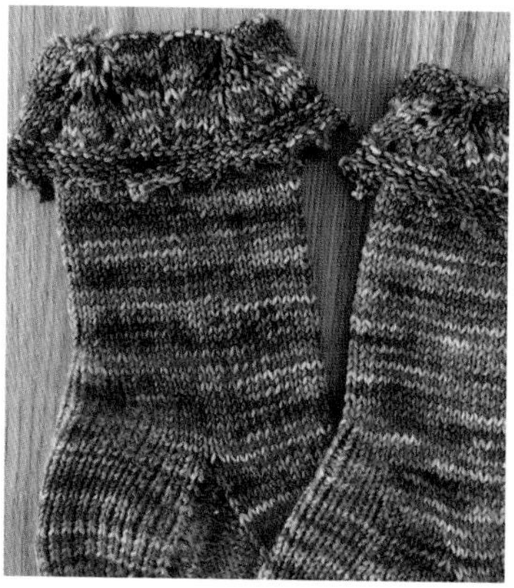

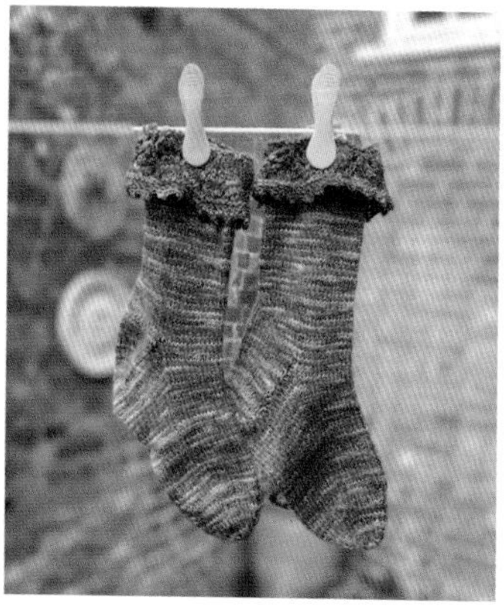

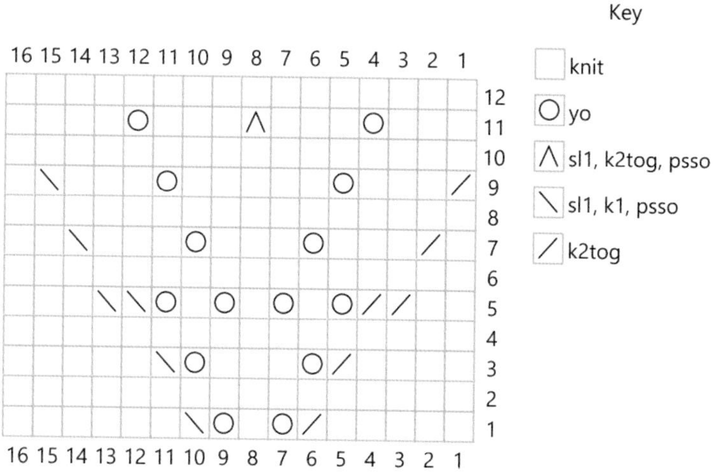

Linnet lace cuff chart.

Materials: 100g [100, 100, 150, 150, 150, 150, 200, 200, 200, 200] 4-ply sock wool. I used Kosy Kitchen Fibres in shade Raspberry Crush.
Foot circumference: 12.5cm [15, 17.5, 18.5, 21, 23.5, 25.5, 27]/5in [6, 7, 7½, 8½, 9½, 10, 10½].
Tension: 32sts and 38 rows to 10cm over st st using 2.75mm needles.

Instructions

Make two socks the same.

Using 2.75mm needles and a provisional cast on, knit 1 round on 40 [44, 48, 52, 56, 60, 64, 68, 72, 76, 80] sts then work 16 rounds of k1 p1 rib.

Cont in st st until leg is required length.

Start heel

Row 1: k10 [11, 12, 13, 14, 15, 16, 17, 18, 19, 20], turn.
Row 2: sl1, p19 [21, 23, 25, 27, 29, 31, 33, 35, 37, 39].

Cont on these sts, slipping the first one of each row until heel measures approx. 8cm/3in.

Shape heel

Row 1: sl1, k10 [11, 12, 13, 14, 15, 16, 17, 18, 19, 20] ssk, k1, turn.
Row 2: sl1, p4, p2tog, p1, turn.
Row 3: sl1, k5, ssk, k1, turn.
Row 4: sl1, p6, p2tog, p1, turn.

Cont working 1 more st each time until all sts have been worked.

Knit to centre of heel for the start of the rounds; pm here if required.

Knit first half of heel sts, pick up and knit 10 [11, 12, 13, 14, 15, 16, 17, 18, 19, 20, 21] sts along side of heel flap, pm1, k instep sts and pm2, pick up and knit 10 [11, 12, 13, 14, 15, 16, 17, 18, 19, 20, 21] sts along other side of heel flap, k to centre of heel.

Knit 1 round.

Shape gusset

K to 2sts before pm1, k2tog, k to pm2, ssk, k to end.

Dec in this way on alt rounds until sts are reduced to original number.

Cont until foot is required length.

Shape toe

Arrange sts on 4 needles with an equal number on each, or, if using a circular needle, place markers at 4 equal distances.

On each needle work (k1, ssk, k to end, k2tog, k1).

Work 3 rounds and rep dec round.

Cont dec until there are 20sts altog, (k1, sk2p, k1) on each needle.

K1 more round then thread yarn through rem sts, draw up and fasten off firmly.

Lace cuff

Lace pattern

Round 1: k5, k2tog, yo, k1, yo, sl1, k1, psso, k6. (16sts)

Round 2: knit.

Round 3: k4, k2tog, yo, k3, yo, sl1, k1, psso, k5.

Round 4: knit.

Round 5: k2, k2tog × 2, (yo, k1) × 3, yo, sl1, k1, psso × 2, k3.

Round 6: knit.

Round 7: k1, k2tog, (k3, yo) × 2, k3, sl1, k1, psso, k2.

Round 8: knit.

Round 9: k2tog, k3, yo, k5, yo, k3, sl1, k1, psso, k1.

Round 10: knit.

Round 11: k3, yo, k3, sl1, k2tog, psso, k3, yo, k4.

Round 12: knit.

Turn sock inside out and with WS facing k1 round inc 8 [4, 0, 12, 8, 4, 0, 12, 8, 4, 0] sts to a multiple of 16 for lace pattern [48, 48, 48, 64, 64, 64, 64, 80, 80, 80] sts.

Work 12 rounds of pattern then 5 rounds of g st.

Work picot cast off as follows: cast off 3, (cast on 2, cast off 5) to end.

Fasten off.

Finishing

Darn in any ends, block and press, turning the lace to the right side.

MALLARD

A fairly basic sock with a longer leg to wear in boots. The cuff is worked in a plain yarn to show off the slightly unusual rib pattern. The rest of the sock, including the Dutch heel, is knitted in a k3 p3 rib to grip the leg closely. The spiral toe is knitted in the plain yarn, again, to make the pattern more of a feature.

Materials: 100g King Cole Zig Zag in shade Coco, plus small amount of plain 4-ply yarn. Circular needles or dpns, sizes 2.25mm and 2.75mm.

Foot size: to fit 20cm [23, 27]/8in [9¼, 10½].

Tension: 30sts and 38 rows to 10cm over rib using 2.75mm needles.

Instructions

Make two socks the same.

Using 2.25mm needles and plain coloured yarn, cast on 60 [69, 78] sts and join to work in the round.

Round 1: k3, p3.

Round 2: k1, p1.

Work these 2 rounds for 14 rounds more.

Change to 2.75mm needles and Zig Zag and work in k3 p3 rib for 20cm/8in.

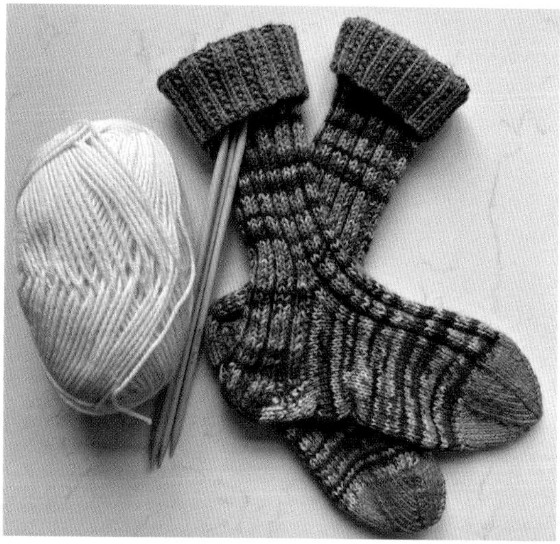

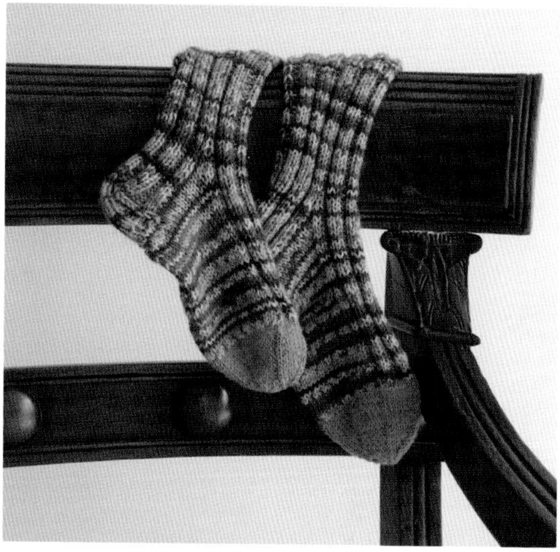

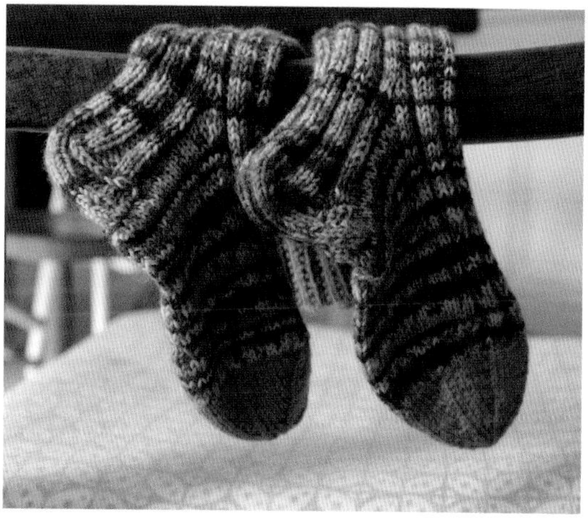

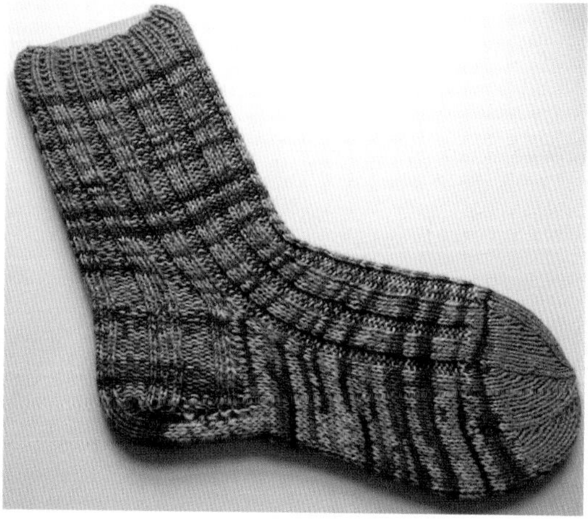

Shape heel

Rib 33 [33, 39] for heel and leave rem sts for instep.

Work 23 rows more.

Turn heel

Row 1: sl1, rib 22 [22, 25] p2tog, turn.
Row 2: sl1, rib 12 [15], ssk, turn.
Cont as for row 2 until all sts are used.

Pick up and knit 15 [15, 18] alongside of heel, rib across instep sts, pick up and knit 15 [15, 18] along other side of heel.

Continue in st st for foot and rib for instep until foot is required length less 6cm/2½in for toe.

Decrease evenly to 66sts for 2nd size.

Change to plain yarn.

Shape toe

*k8 [9, 11], k2tog; repeat from * to end.
Work 1 round.
*k7 [8, 10], k2tog; repeat from * to end.

Cont decreasing on alt rounds until sts are reduced to 6.

Thread yarn through, draw up firmly and fasten off.

Finishing

Darn in all ends. Block and press.

PARTRIDGE

This is a basic medium-sized sock knitted in stocking stitch using variegated or self-striping yarn but with a solid colour yarn for the cuff, heel and toe. The heel is knitted in Eye of Partridge stitch, a basic slip stitch but with the slipped stitches alternating on every right-side row. It is a more hard-wearing heel but is not as rigid as some slipped stitch heels can be. Eye of Partridge stitch shows up best in a solid colour so if the main yarn is variegated choose another yarn for the heel, cuff and toe. The toe is shaped by working evenly spaced decreases until all stitches are worked off. This avoids grafting for those who don't like it. Most of the toes in this book can be worked in this way over an even number of stitches.

Materials: 100g 4-ply sock yarn in main colour (MC); 50g contrast yarn (C) (optional). Needles: size 2.75mm.
Size: to fit UK size 5 or 6 with a foot circumference of 20cm/8in.
Tension: 30sts and 42 rounds on 2.5mm needles to 10cm/4in.

Instructions

Make two socks the same.

Using the contrast yarn, provisionally cast on 12sts and work in g st until cuff fits around leg at the height required. Undo any waste yarn and graft the two edges together.

Join into a circle, being careful not to twist the stitches.

Pick up and knit 60sts from edge of cuff.

Knit for approximately 40 rounds or desired length of sock.

Heel flap

Place 30sts on a spare needle or stitch holder for the instep. Continue on the other half of the stitches for the heel flap and work in Partridge stitch for 28 rows.

Partridge stitch

Row 1 (RS): *sl1, k1*, repeat from * ending with k1.
Row 2 and all even rows: sl1, purl.
Row 3: sl2, * k1, sl1*, repeat from * ending with k2.
Row 4: repeat row 2.

Turn heel

Row 1: sl1, p 16 p2tog, p1, turn.
Row 2: sl1, k5, ssk, k1, turn.
Row 3: sl1, p6, p2tog, p1, turn.
Row 4: sl1, k7, ssk, k1, turn.
Row 5: sl1, p8, p2tog, p1, turn.
Row 6: sl1, k9, ssk, k1, turn.
Row 7: sl1, p10, p2tog, p1, turn.
Row 8: sl1, k11, ssk, k1, turn.
Row 9: sl1, p12, p2tog, p1, turn.

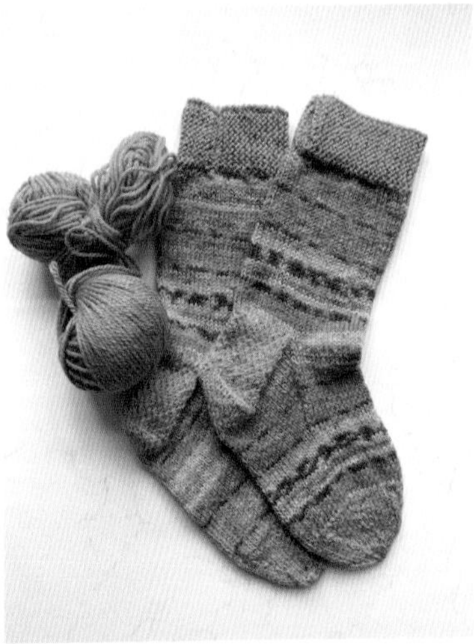

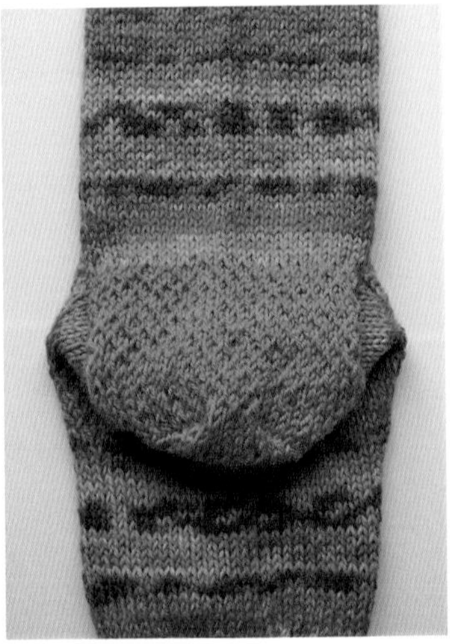

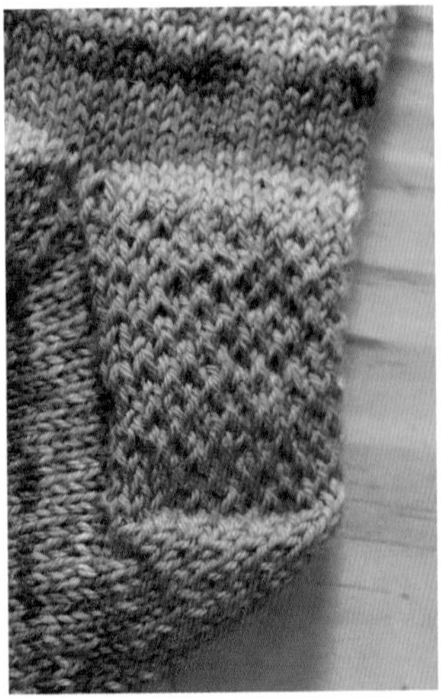

Row 10: sl1, k13, ssk, k1, turn.
Row 11: sl1, p14, p2tog, p1, turn.
Row 12: k16, ssk, k1. (18sts)

If using a contrast yarn for heel, break off the contrast. Using MC pick up and knit 15sts alongside of heel flap, inc in bar bet sts, knit next 30sts from those left on holder, inc in bar, pick up and knit 15sts along other side of heel flap, then k9 from heel. The next stitch will be the start of the round.

K2 rounds on all 80 stitches placing stitch markers after 15 and 30 stitches.

Gusset

Round 1: k to 3sts before first marker, k2tog, k 1, k30sts to next marker k1, ssk, k to end.
Round 2: knit.
Rep these 2 rounds until 60sts remain and cont for foot working 42 rounds or number required for length of foot minus section for toe.

Toe

Change to contrast yarn if required.
Round 1: (ssk, k8) 6 times.
Knit 2 rounds.
Round 4: (k2tog, k7) 6 times.
Knit 2 rounds.
Round 7: (k2tog, k6) 6 times.
Knit 2 rounds.

Cont in this way working 1 less st bet decreases to:
Round 18: (k2tog, k1) 6 times.
Knit 1 round.

Finishing

Cut yarn, leaving a short tail about 20cm/8in long. Thread the tail end into a tapestry needle and draw it through the remaining 12 stitches twice. Tighten and fasten off firmly. Darn in any ends. Block and press.

PHOENIX

A variegated flamboyant yarn such as this needs very little embellishment, but I have added a simple eyelet pattern at the top of the sock for extra interest. The pattern is written for four sizes and is best worked on a set of double-pointed needles, at least for the toe section. The rest could be worked on a circular needle if preferred. The heel is worked in stocking stitch and features the German short row technique. The rest of the foot is continued in stocking stitch. The toe is an interesting feature and is worked by decreasing to give a comfortable rounded shape, finished off by threading the yarn through the remaining stitches and drawing the hole closed. So no grafting to do!

Materials: 100g [150, 200, 250] 4-ply sock wool. These were knitted using Skein Queen Crush in shade Tropical Toucan.
Foot size: 15cm [18.5, 23.5, 27]/6in [7½, 9½, 10½].
Tension: 32sts and 40 rows to 10cm over st st using 2.75mm needles.

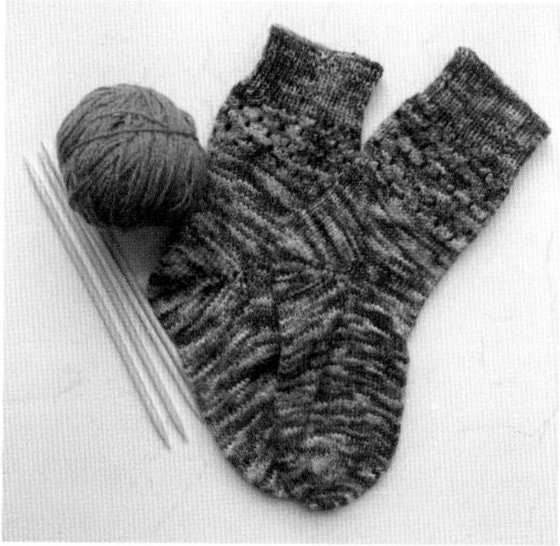

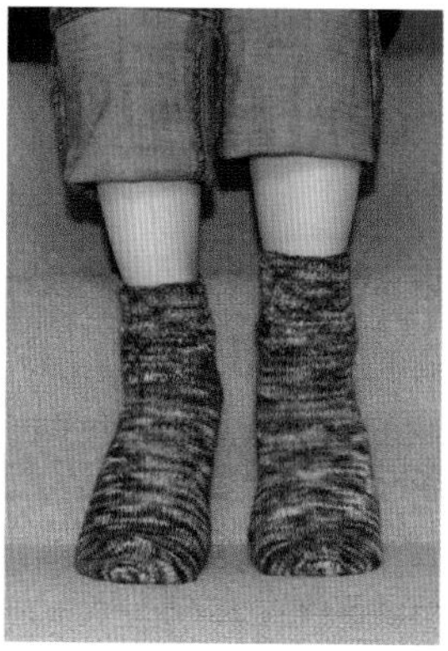

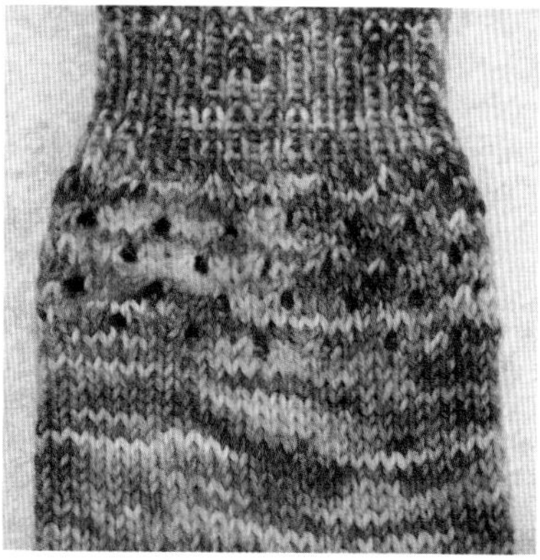

Lace pattern

Round 1: (k2, k2tog, yf) to end.
Knit 2 rounds.
Round 4: (k2tog, yf, k2) to end.
Knit 2 rounds.

Instructions

Make two socks the same.
Using 2.75mm needles, cast on 40 [48, 56, 64] sts and join to work in the round.
Work 5cm/2in k1 p1 rib.
Work in lace pattern for 6cm/2.5in then cont in st st until work measures 20cm/8in or length required then shape heel.

German short row heel

Knit 20 [24, 28, 32] sts, divide the work into 3, placing stitch markers at the divisions.

If the numbers are not equal the two outer sections should have the same number of stitches as each other and the centre section will have one more or one fewer stitches.

Row 1: with yarn at front, slip the first stitch, pull the yarn firmly so that the stitch rolls around the needle and 2 loops lie on the needle, purl to end, turn.
Row 2 and all following rows: as for row 1, working as far as the double stitch before turning. Bring yarn to front each time before making the double stitch and remember to take it back before working a knit row.
When all of the outer stitches have been turned into double stitches (ds) and the right side is facing work on all of the sts, incl those left on holder for the instep working each of the doubled stitches as though they were one stitch.
Now work back across the stitches, making a ds as before in the first stitch after a turn.
So the next row will be ds, k to first ds, knit that stitch plus one more, turn.

Continue in this way until all the turns and double stitches have been made and the last stitch is a double stitch. Knit that stitch then continue to work in the round until foot measures 12.5cm [15.25, 20.25, 23]/5in [6, 8, 9].

Three-point toe

Increase/decrease stitches where necessary to a multiple of three.

There will now be 42 [48, 57, 63] sts. Arrange these stitches onto 3 needles so that each needle has the same number.

Decrease one stitch at the beginning and end of each needle on alt rounds until there are 5 stitches left on each one.

Thread yarn through the rem stitches, draw up firmly to close the hole and fasten off.

Finishing

Darn in any ends. Block and press.

SERIN

These are toe up socks started with Turkish or Judy's Magic cast on. The sole is worked in stocking stitch with the instep and leg in Old Shale. When the foot is long enough to reach the point at which the ankle turns, work increases for a Fleegle heel and then continue working Old Shale all around the leg for the length required. Change to one size smaller needles and work a cuff in your choice of rib.

Materials: 100g 4-ply sock wool. Kosy Kitchen Fibres in shade English Country Garden.
Needles, dpns or circular sizes 2.25mm and 2.75mm.
Foot circumference: 19cm [23]/7½in [9].
Tension: 30sts and 42 rows using 2.75mm needles over st st.

Old Shale pattern (multiple of 11sts)

Round 1: k3, (k2tog) × 2 *(yo, k1) × 3, yo (k2tog) × 4: rep from * ending (k2tog) × 2, k3.
Rounds 2 & 3: knit.
Round 4: purl.

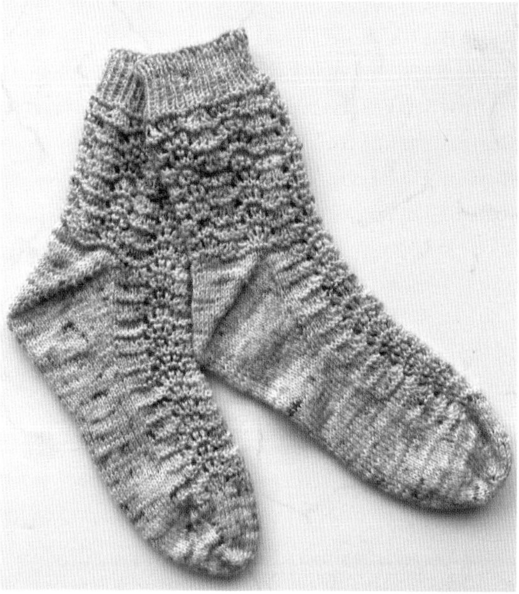

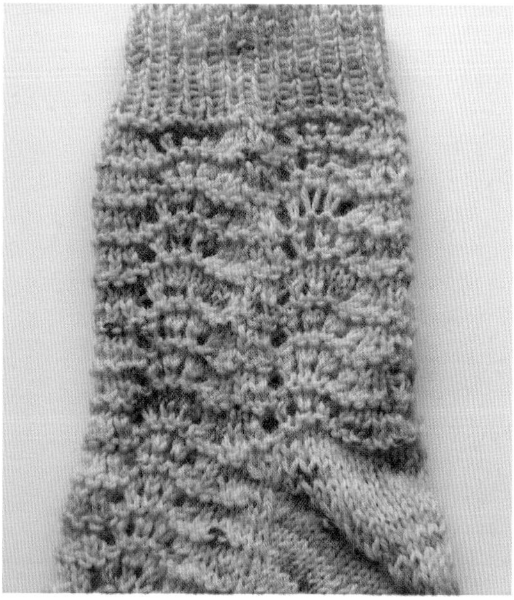

Round 5: knit.
Rep these 5 rounds.

Begin at toe

Using Turkish or Judy's Magic Cast On and two 2.5mm needles or one circular needle, cast on 6 stitches (3 on each needle).

Knit 1 round.
Next round: Inc in every stitch (12sts).
Next round: inc 1 st at beg and end of each needle, 1 stitch in from the edge (16sts).
Work 2 rounds.
Repeat the last 3 rounds once more (24sts).
Inc as before in next and every foll alt row to 56 [66] sts.
When toe measures 6cm/2½in divide sts over 3 needles with 28 [34] on needle 1 and 14 [16] on needles 2 and 3.
Work Old Shale over first needle and st st over the others.
Repeat the 5 rounds until foot is required length less 6cm/2.5in for heel.

Continue to knit in the round and work in pattern over instep stitches.

Begin Fleegle heel

In next and every alternate round, inc 1 at beg needle 2 and end of needle 3 by working a lifted increase as follows:

Knit 1st stitch, lift stitch on row below and knit into right leg of it. On needle 3, lift stitch on row below and knit into left leg of it, knit the last stitch.

When there are 27 [32] sts on each of needles 2 and 3 slip all of these stitches onto one needle. Mark the centre stitch.

Knit one round keeping the pattern correct over the instep.

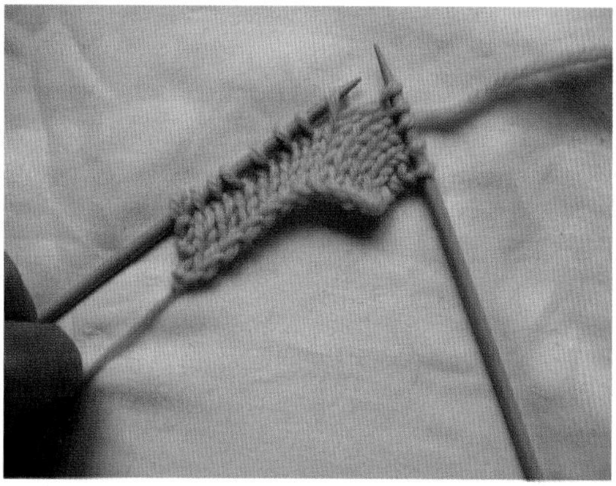

A m1L lifted increase to make an extra stitch to the left.

Turn the heel

K26 [31], k2tog, k26 [31]

Next row: k past centre st, k2tog, k1, turn.

Next row: sl1, p past centre st, p2togtbl, p1, turn.

Rep these 2 rows until sts are reduced to 55 [66].

Slip 3 [6] to end of previous needle and work in rounds of Old Shale pattern until leg is required length.

Change to size smaller needle and work ribbed cuff for 15 rounds.

Cast off loosely.

Finishing

Darn in any ends. Block and press.

SPECKLED HEN

Pretty socks worked top down with a frilly top to the cuff made using a picot cast on. The leg and top of the foot are knitted in a lacy pattern to resemble feathers. The socks have a basic flap and gusset heel but the toe is slightly unusual in that it swirls over three points to give a spiral effect.

Materials: 100g Hiddleston 4-ply sock wool from Mr B's yarns at Birdstreet Uk. Shade Bonfire Night. Needles: set of 4 dpns or circular needle size 2.75mm. 2 stitch markers.

Foot circumference: 20cm/8in.

Tension: 32sts and 40 rows to 10cm over st st using 2.75mm needles.

Feather Lace

Round 1: p1, k10, k2tog, yo, k1, p2. (16sts)

Round 2: p1, k9, k2tog, k2, yo, p2.

Round 3: k9, k2tog, k1, yo, k2, p2.

Round 4: k8, k2tog, k3, yo, k1, p2.

Round 5: k7, k2tog, k2, yo, k3, p2.

Round 6: k6, k2tog, k4, yo, k2, p2.

Round 7: k5, k2tog, k3, yo, k4, p2.

Round 8: k4, k2tog, k5, yo, k3, p2.

Round 9: k2, yo, ssk, k10, p2.

Round 10: k1, yo, k2, ssk, k9, p2.

Round 11: k3, yo, k1, ssk, k8, p2.

Round 12: k2, yo, k3, ssk, k7, p2.

Round 13: k4, yo, k2, ssk, k6, p2.

Round 14: k3, yo, k4, ssk, k5, p2.

Round 15: k5, yo, k3, ssk, k4, p2.

Round 16: k4, yo, k5, ssk, k3, p2.

Instructions

Make two socks the same.

Using 2.75mm needles and cable cast on; *cast on 5, cast off 2; rep from * to 62sts, cast on 2 (64sts).

Knit 3 rounds.

Work 12 rounds in k2, p2 rib.

Continue in Feather lace pattern following chart or written instructions until leg measures length required.

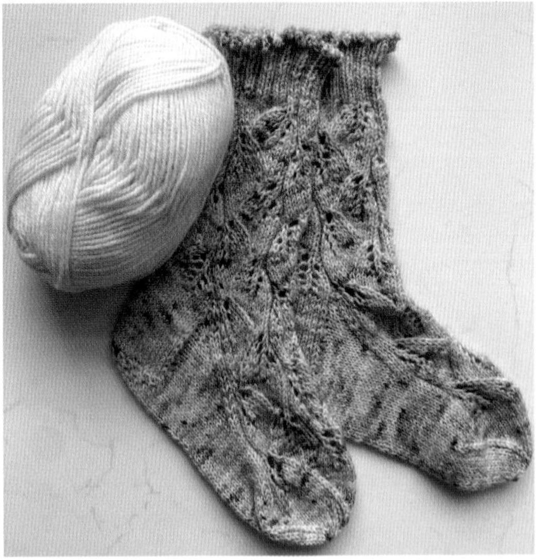

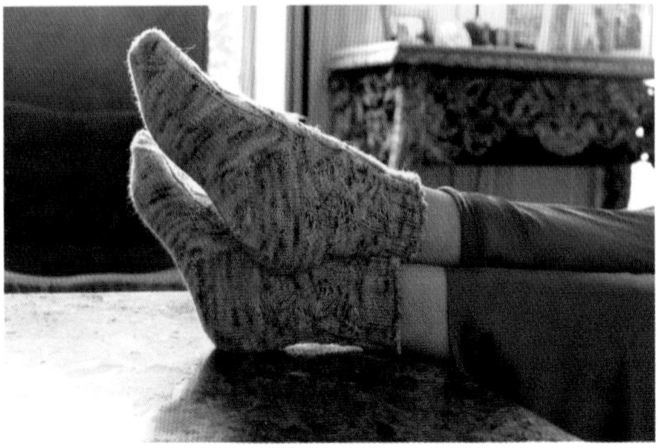

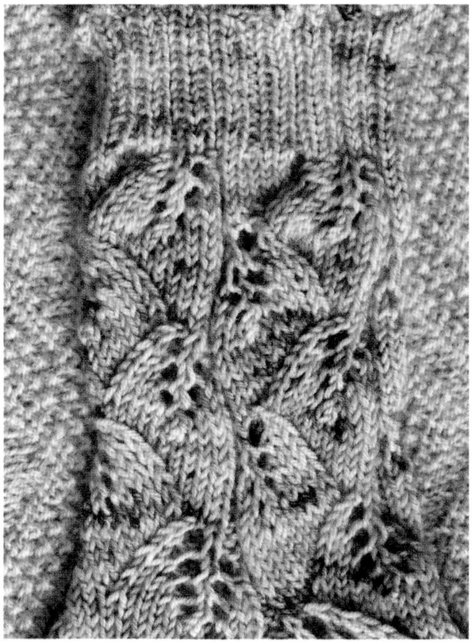

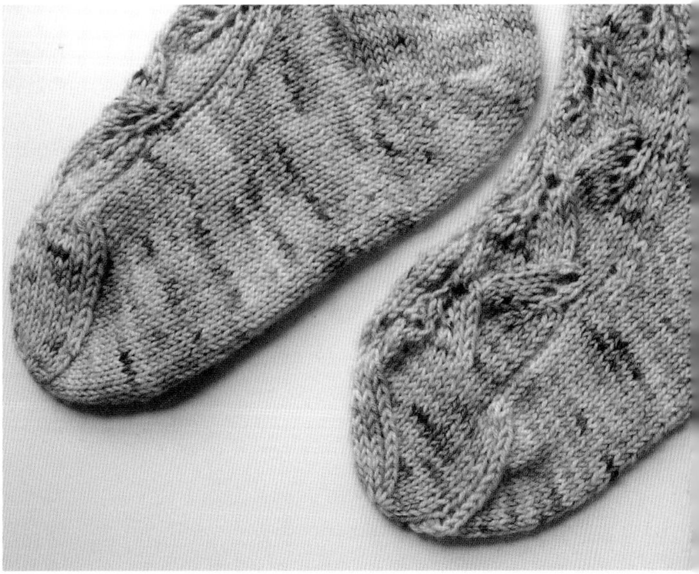

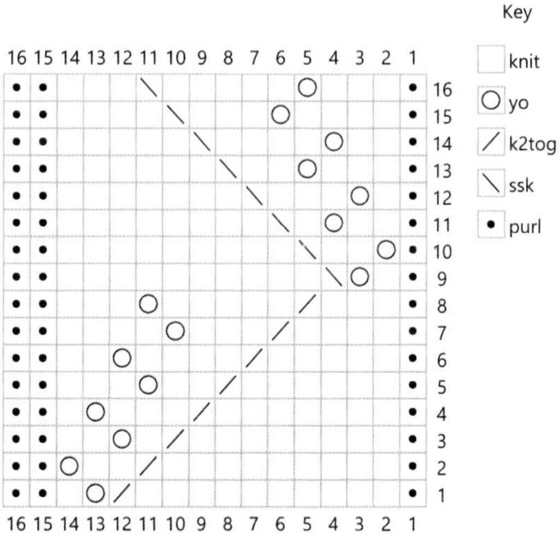

Speckled Hen chart.

Shape heel

K16, turn, p16; leave rem 32sts for instep and cont on heel sts for 6cm/2½in ending after a WS row.

Row 1: sl 1, k17, ssk, k1, turn.
Row 2: sl1, p5, p2togp1, turn.
Row 3: sl1, k6, ssk, k1, turn.
Row 4: sl1, p7, p2tog, p1, turn.

Cont in this way, working 1 more st before decreasing each time, until all sts are used.

Knit across all sts then pick up and knit 16sts along sides of heel flap, pattern across 32 instep sts, pick up and knit 16 along other side of heel flap, knit 9 from heel (this is the start of each round). Place markers at beg and end of instep sts.

Knit to 3sts before 1st marker, k2tog, k1, pattern across instep sts to 2nd marker, k1, ssk.

Work 1 more round.

Repeat decrease round until 64sts remain.

Continue in pattern until foot is required length less 6cm/2½in.

Decrease to 63sts on last round.

Shape toe

Place 21sts on each of 3 needles.

Work ssk at beg of each needle until there are 12sts altogether.

Thread yarn through rem sts, draw up and fasten off firmly.

Finishing

Darn in any ends. Block and press.

SPIRAL SOCKS

These socks have no shaping apart from at the toe and are useful to wear with boots or as bedsocks. They can be made in any DK or Aran weight yarn and are useful for using up stash. Use size 4mm needles for DK or 4.5mm needles if working in Aran. They are one size but a different multiple of 8 stitches will make them larger or smaller.

Materials: 200g any DK or Aran yarn. Needles: a set of 4 dpns or a circular needle size 4mm for DK or 4.5mm for Aran. A tapestry needle.
Size: Small [medium, large, extra large]
Tension: 22sts and 28 rows with DK on size 4mm needles to 10cm/4in. 18sts and 24 rows with Aran.

Instructions

Make two socks the same.

Cast on 48 [56, 64, 72] sts and work 12 rounds of k4 p4 rib.

Start spiral pattern

Round 1: p1, *k4, p4; repeat from * ending last repeat p3.
Work 3 more rounds as set.
Round 5: p2, *k4, p4; repeat from * ending last repeat, p2.
Work 3 more rounds as set.
Round 9: p3, *k4, p4; repeat from * ending last repeat p1.
Work 3 more rounds as set.
Round 13: * p4, K4; repeat from * to end.
Work 3 more rounds as set.

Continue in this way for length required, moving pattern one stitch every 8th round, until the sock measures approx. 6cm/2½in short of the toe.

Shape toe

Continue in st st.

Round 1: (k6, k2tog), to end.
Rounds 2 & 3: knit.
Round 4: (k5, k2tog) to end.
Rounds 5 & 6: knit.
Round 7: (k4, k2tog) to end.
Round 8: knit.
Round 9: (k3, k2tog) to end.
Round 10: knit.
Round 11: (k2, k2tog) to end.
Round 12: (k1, k2tog) to end.
Round 13: k2tog to end.

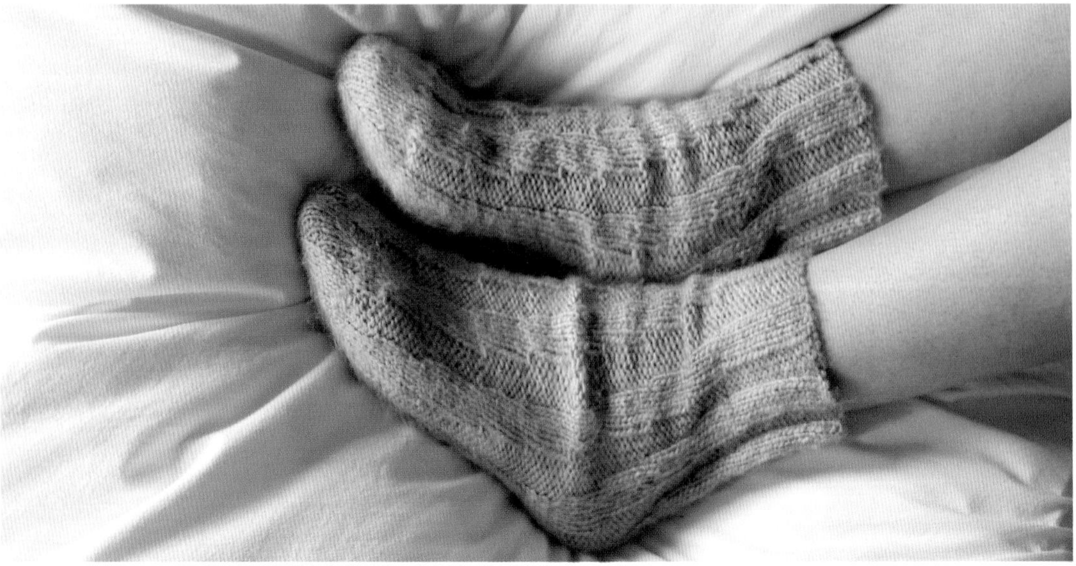

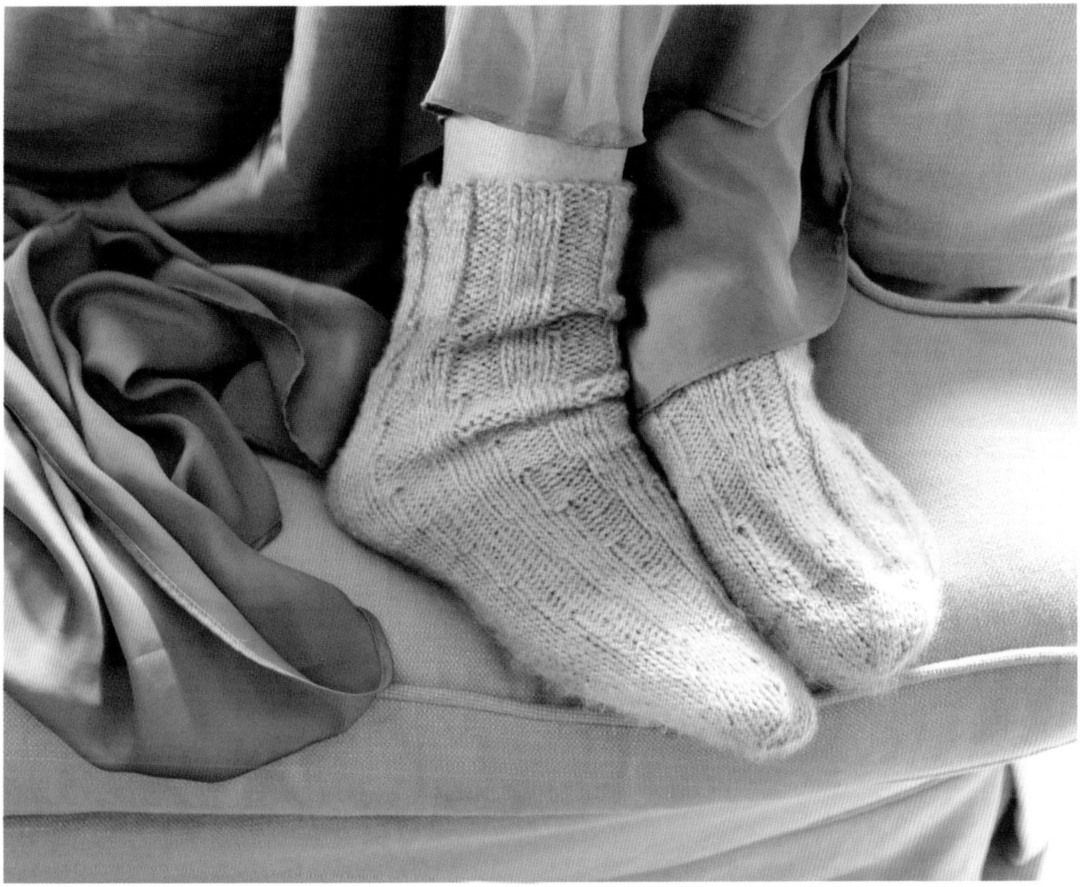

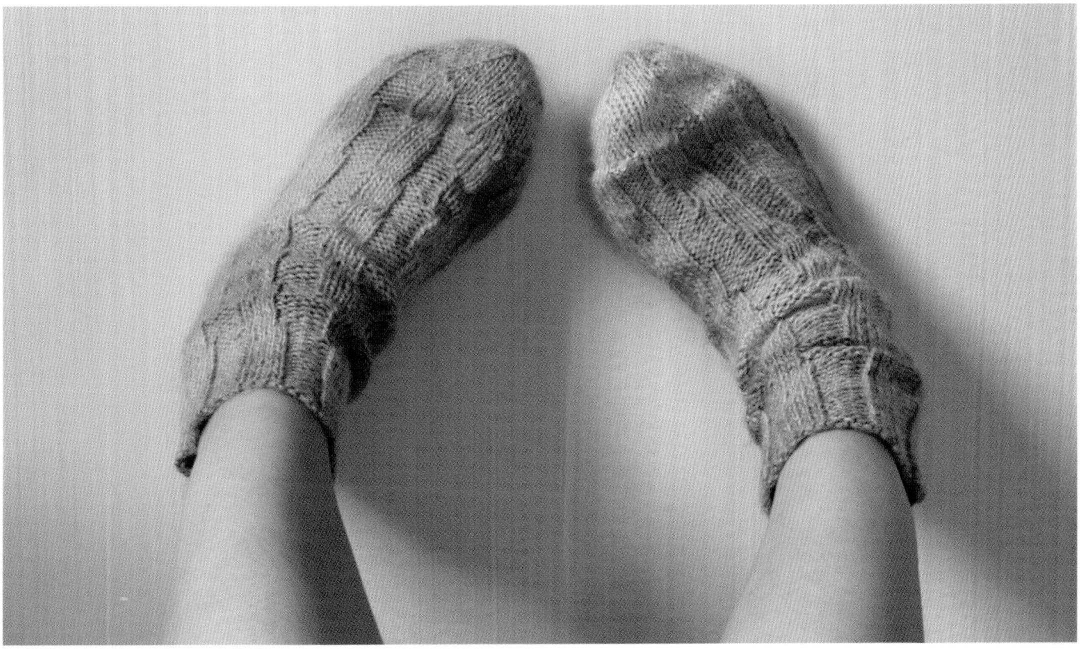

Thread yarn through rem sts, draw up and fasten off firmly.

To make a firmer closure, thread yarn through last round again and draw up. Break off yarn and darn in on inside.

SWIFT

These socks are worked from the toe up in stocking stitch apart from a deep band of lace below the cuff. The lace pattern is a multiple of 16sts but you may like to substitute a pattern of your choice that will fit neatly into 48sts.

Materials: Malabrigo Sock 100 per cent Superwash Merino Wool, 402m (440yds) per 100g skein. Needles size 3.00mm.

Size: to fit woman's medium foot.

Tension: 28sts and 38 rows to 10cm/4in on 3.00mm needles.

Lace pattern

Round 1: p5, yo, ssk, k3, k2tog, yo, p4. (16sts)
Round 2: p5, k7, p4.
Round 3: p3, p2tog, yo, k1, yo, ssk, k1, k2tog, yo, k1, yo, p2tog, p2.
Round 4: p4, k9, p3.
Round 5: p2, p2tog, yo, k3, yo, sl1, k2tog, psso, yo, k3, yo, p2tog, p1.
Round 6: p3, k11, p2.
Round 7: p1, p2tog, yo, k11, yo, p2tog.
Round 8: repeat round 6.
Round 9: p3, yo, ssk, k7, k2tog, yo, p2.
Round 10: repeat round 4.
Round 11: p4, yo, ssk, k5, k2tog, yo, p3.
Round 12: repeat round 2.

Instructions

Make two socks the same.

Cast on 11sts onto one needle, using the thumb method and knit 4 rows.

Leave these sts on 1st needle and with 2nd needle, pick up and knit 11sts along the other side of the cast on stitches. Knit 1 round on all 22sts.

Continue working in rounds. To avoid holes or slackness, give the first two stitches of each

TIP

It can sometimes be difficult to pick up and knit cast on stitches. Slip them onto a finer needle first and then knit them off onto the correct size.

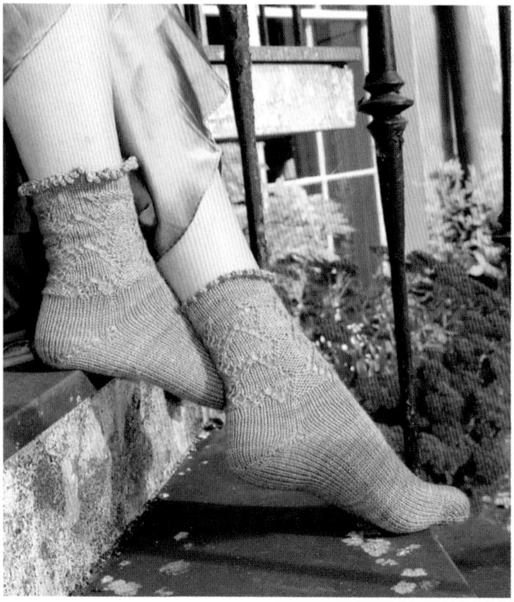

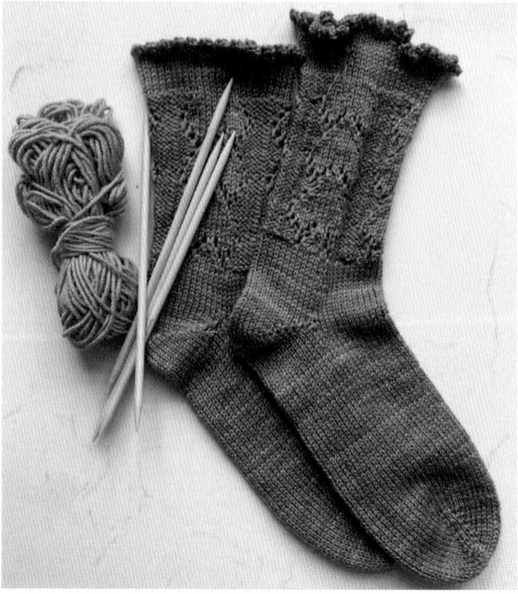

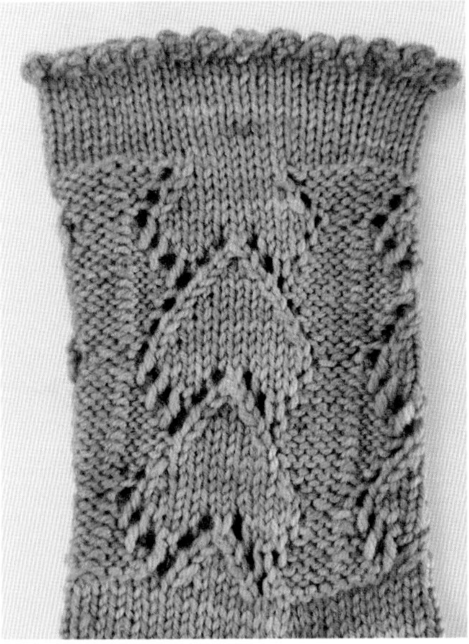

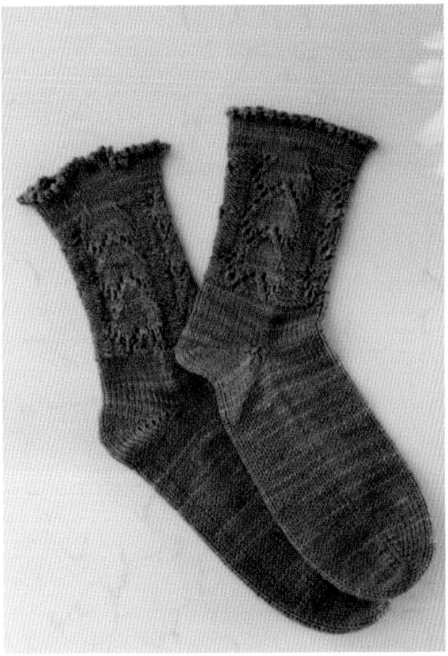

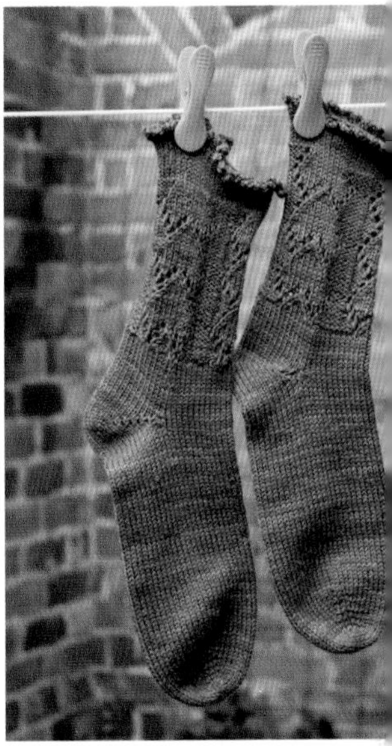

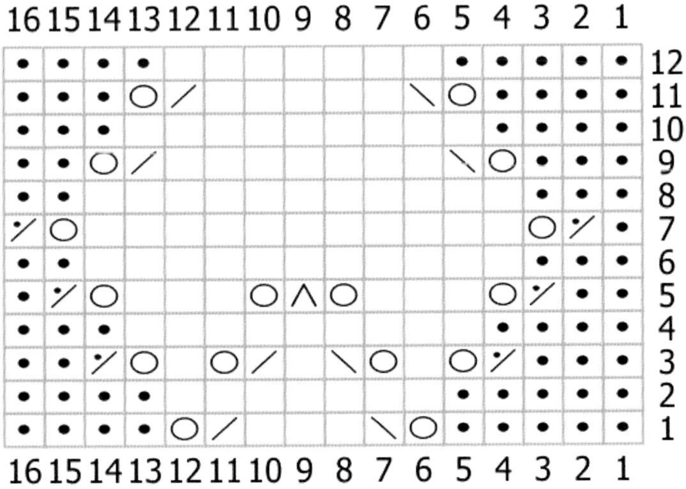

Swift chart.

Key

- knit
- purl
- yo
- ssk
- k2tog
- p2tog
- sl1, k2tog, psso

needle a firm tug before proceeding to the end. Inc 1 st at each end of both needles on alternate rows until there are 50sts.

Mark the centre stitches on the sole and instep to make it easier to centre the heel shaping based on these markers.

Slip last 13sts just worked onto 3rd needle then k4 onto same needle.

Work in rounds for approx. 18cm/7in, or length required for foot.

Try sock on at this point, being careful not to lose any of the stitches. The heel will require approximately 2 more inches.

Fleegle heel shaping

Starting with a purl row, slip last 4 stitches of the round onto 1st needle, knit 17 then knit 4 from the 2nd needle (25sts).

Work in rows, slipping the first st of every row and leaving the last st of every row unworked until there are 11 live sts left at the centre ending with a RS row.

Next row: sl1, p10, lift the stitch below next one and place it onto the needle then ptogtbl with next st.

Next row: sl1, k11, lift st as before, place it on needle and knit it tog with next st.

Rep these 2 rows working one more stitch each time until all 25sts are back in work.

Finish the round by working across the stitches left for the instep with 17sts on 2 needles and 16 on the third (50sts).

Cont until heel measures 3cm/1¼in, or depth required, then, on next round, k2tog at centre of each of needles 1 and 2 (48sts).

Knit 1 round then work lace pattern for 36 rounds. (It may be necessary to redistribute the sts over the needles to make it easier to work the decreases.)

Knit 10 rounds.

Work picot cast off

Cast off 2; *insert needle into next st and cast on 3; cast off 5; rep from * to end.

Finishing

Fasten off yarn and darn in all ends. Block and press.

TURNSTONE

A cosy pair of socks with a cabled top that turns over onto the ribbed leg. The cuff is knitted sideways, joined into a circle and then stitches are picked up along the edge to work downwards to the flap and gusset heel. The heel is turned by working one more stitch at each turn, creating a triangular shaped French heel and the toe is a simple wedge.

The socks could be knitted in a thicker wool, picking up one stitch for every alternate row along the cuff to give a multiple of 6 stitches. Work on half that number of stitches for the heel flap.

Materials: 100g [100, 100, 150, 150] 4-ply sock wool. These were knitted using Kosy Kitchen Fibres sock wool in shade Pebble Beach. Pair 3.00mm needles; circular or dpn needles size 2.75mm.

Foot circumference: 18cm [19.5, 21, 22 ½, 25]/7in [7¾, 8¼, 9, 10].

Tension: 34sts and 40 rows to 10cm over st st using 2.75mm needles.

Cable pattern

Row 1 (RS): p1, k2, p5, k8, p5, k2, p1. (24sts)

Row 2 (WS): k1, p2, k5, 2/2 LC, 2/2 RC, k5, p2, k1.

Row 3: repeat row 1.

Row 4: k1, p2, k3, 2/2 LPC, p4, 2/2 RPC, k3, p2, k1.

Row 5: p1, k2, p3, k2, p2, k4, p2, k2, p3, k2, p1.

Row 6: k1, p2, k1, 2/2 LPC x 2, 2/2 RPC x 2, k1, p2, k1.

Row 7: (p1, k2) × 2, p2, k2, p4, k2, p2, (k2, p1) × 2.

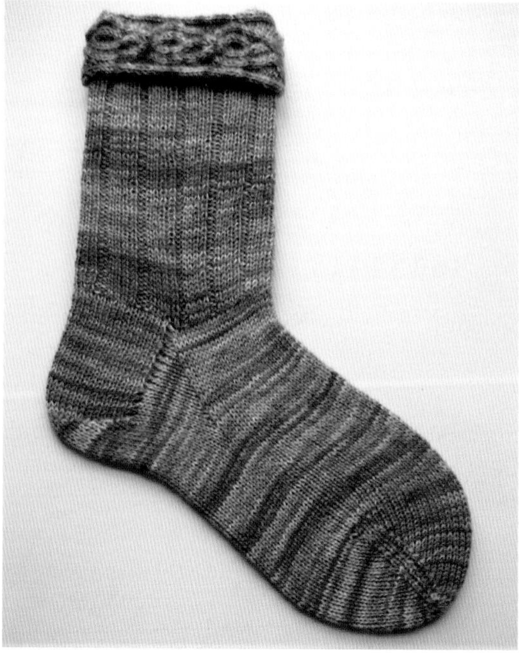

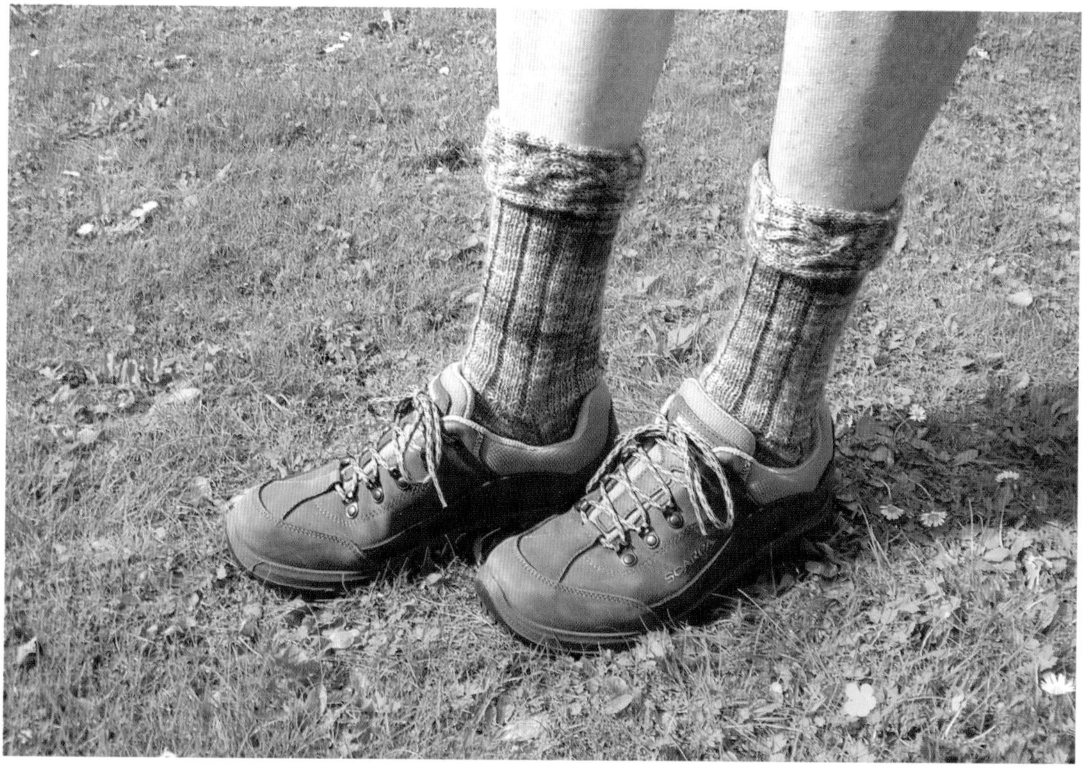
SCARPA

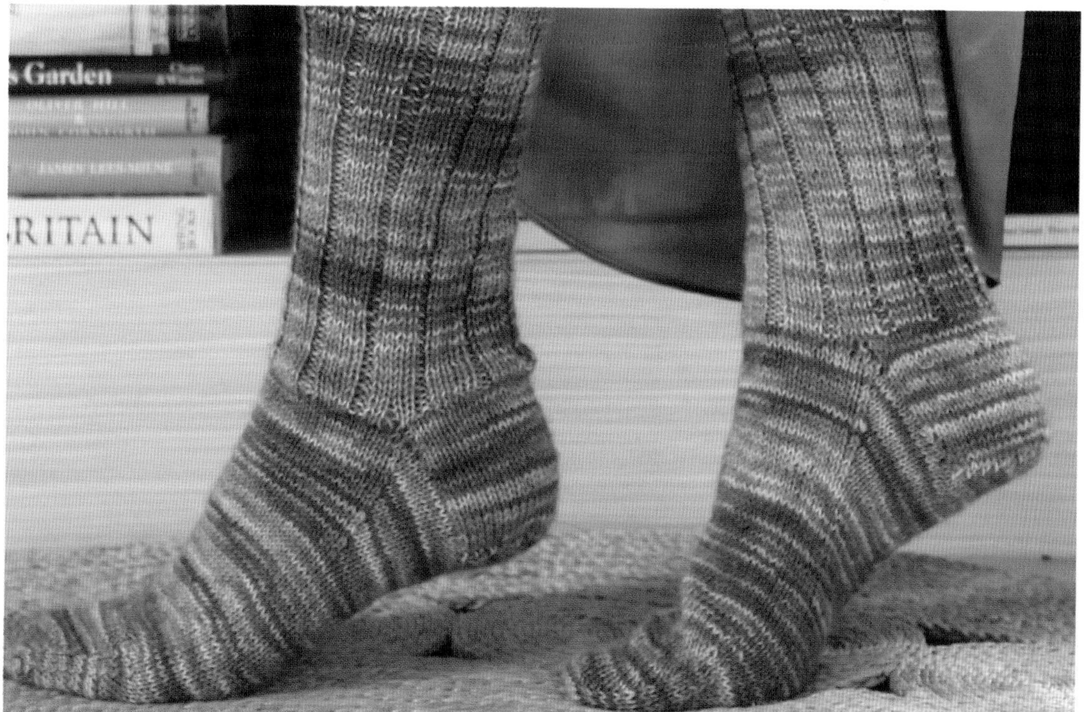
s Garden
RITAIN

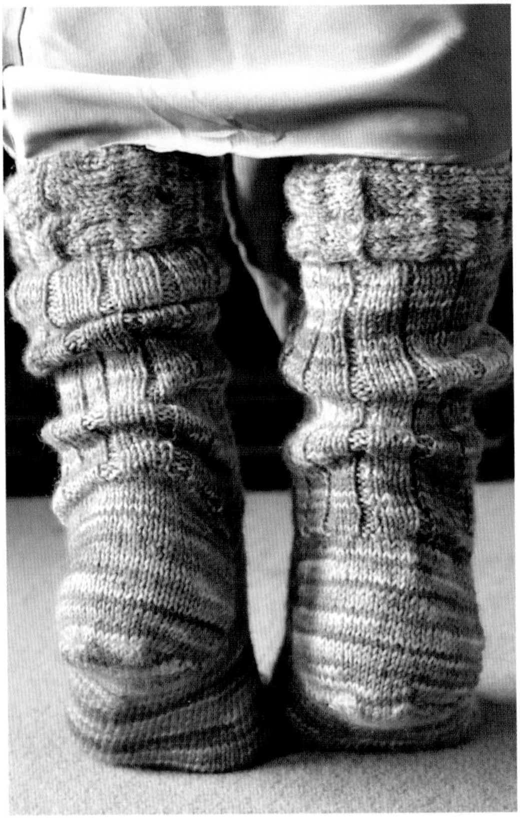

Row 8: (k1, p2) × 2, k2, p2, k4, p2, k2, (p2, k1) × 2.
Row 9: repeat row 7.
Row 10: k1, p2, k1, 2/2 RPC × 2, 2/2 LPC × 2, k1, p2, k1.
Row 11: repeat row 5.
Row 12: k1, p2, k3, p2, k2, 2/2 LC, k2, p2, k3, p2, k1.
Row 13: repeat row 5.
Row 14: k1, p2, k3, 2/2 RPC, p4, 2/2 LPC, k3, p2, k1.
Row 15: repeat row 1.
Row 16: k1, p2, k5, 2/2 RC, 2/2 LC, k5, p2, k1.

Instructions

Make two socks the same.

Cuff

Using 3.00mm needles and a provisional cast on, make 24 stitches. Knit 1 row then work cable pattern from chart or written instructions until band will fit comfortably around leg at the point where you want the socks to start. Join the cuff into a ring by grafting or casting off the stitches together.

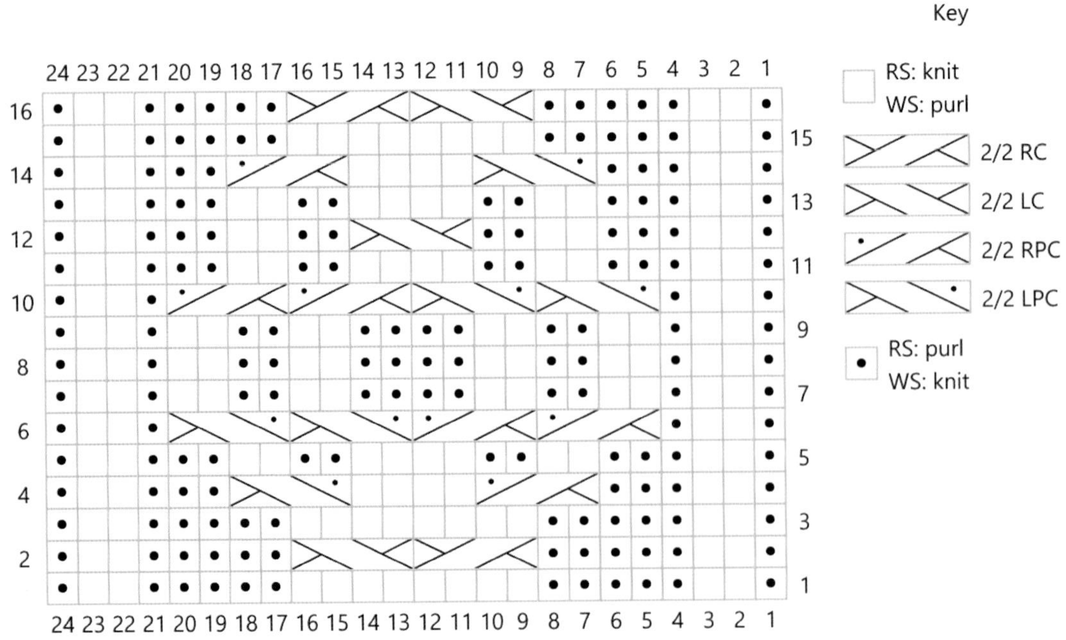

Turnstone chart.

With wrong side facing and using 2.75mm needles, pick up 60 [66, 72, 78, 84] sts along one edge of the cuff beginning at the point where the work was joined.

Now work in k4, p2 rib until leg is required length.

Start heel

Row 1: sl1, k14 [15, 17, 18, 19], turn.
Row 2: p30 [32, 36, 38, 40], turn.
Work 26 rows on these 30 [32, 36, 38, 40] sts.

Shape heel

Row 1: sl1, k17 [18, 19, 20, 21], ssk, k1, turn.
Row 2: sl1, p5, p2tog, p1, turn.
Row 3: sl1, k6, ssk, k1, turn.
Row 4: sl1, p7, p2tog, p1, turn.

Cont in this way, working 1 more stitch between dec and turns until all sts are used.

Knit across half of the heel sts, pick up and knit 15sts alongside of heel, m1, knit across instep sts, m1, pick up and knit 15 along other side of heel, knit the rem heel sts; this is the start of the rounds.

Knit 1 round, placing markers on each of the made sts.

Shape gusset

Knit to 4sts before 1st sm, k2tog, k to 2nd sm, ssk, k to end of round.
Knit 1 round.
Rep last 2 rounds to 60 [66, 72, 78, 84] sts.

Cont until foot is required length minus 6cm/2½in for toe.

Toe

Knit to 1st sm, k2tog, k1, ssk, k to 2nd sm, k2tog, k1, ssk, k to end of round.
Knit 3 rounds.
Rep dec round.
Knit 2 rounds, rep dec round.
Knit 1 round, rep dec round.
Dec on every alt round to 16 [18, 20, 22, 22] sts.
Graft or cast off tog on wrong side.

Finishing

Darn in all ends. Block and press.

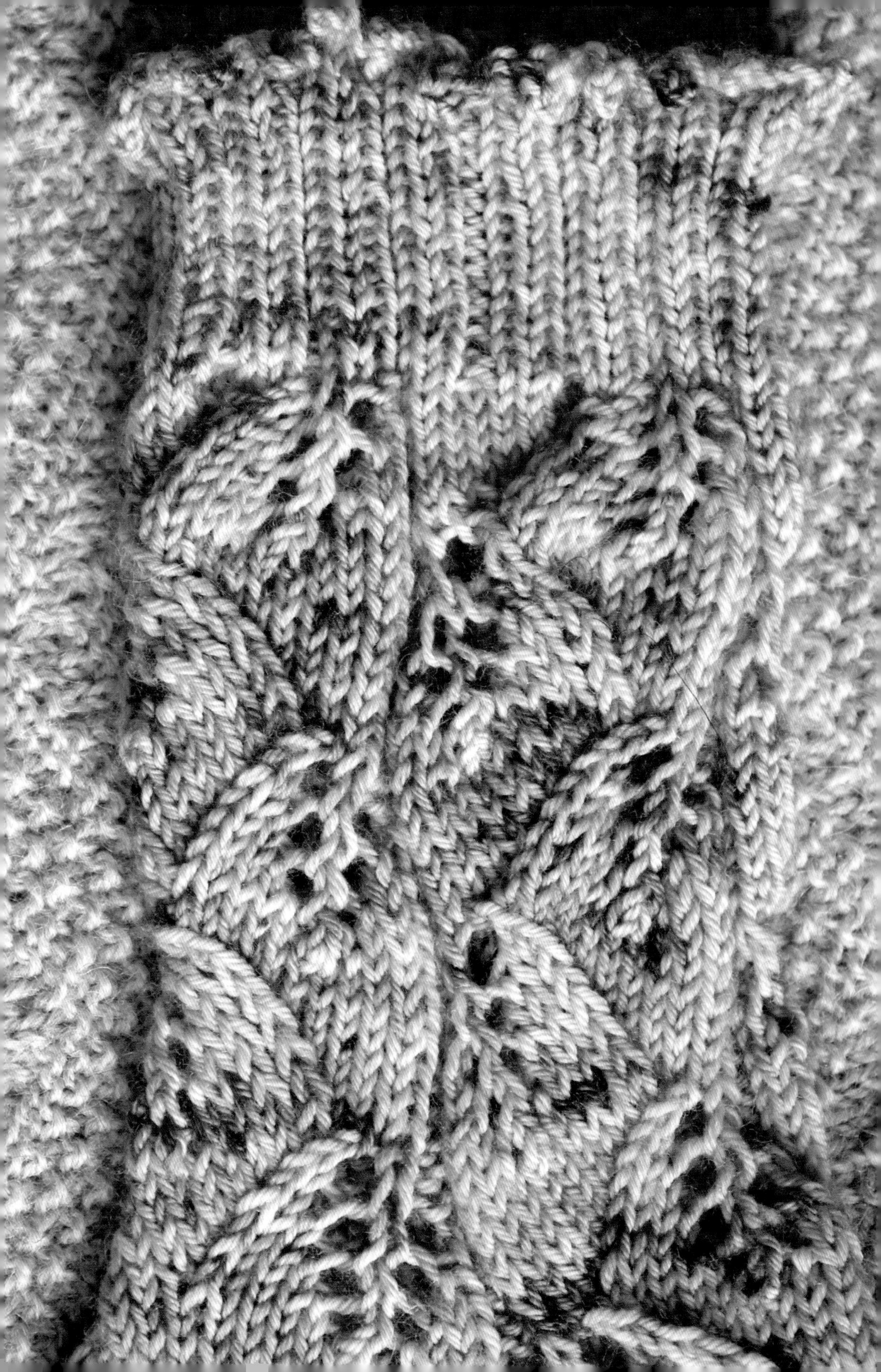

CHAPTER 6

Now Create Your Own

Socks are popular knitting projects because they don't take much yarn so are quick and relatively inexpensive to make. If you have followed the pattern for the basic sock you can easily adapt it by adding lace or cable patterns to make one of your own design. Once you have learnt the basic construction methods the rest should be relatively easy. Don't make it too complicated at first and try out a few test samples to make sure you are happy with the finish.

A sock needs to fit closely and comfortably; you don't want positive ease in a sock or it will ruck up into your shoe or keep falling down your leg. The cuff should grip the leg firmly but not so tight that it constricts the blood flow! It should be smooth around the heel and under the foot, but these parts can be strengthened to avoid too much wear. They are frequently worked in stocking stitch as is the toe. Remember these points when designing your socks.

An average sized sock will require approximately 300m of 4-ply yarn. To begin, take your chosen yarn and needles and make a swatch. For a firm fabric that will wear well it is often best to use a smaller sized needle than that recommended on the ball band. To be absolutely accurate, make the swatch in the round if the socks are to be knitted in the round. And if the main part of the sock is to be knitted in a pattern, knit another swatch in the pattern stitch. Check the number of stitches and rows to 10cm/4in in both swatches. Make a note of these numbers.

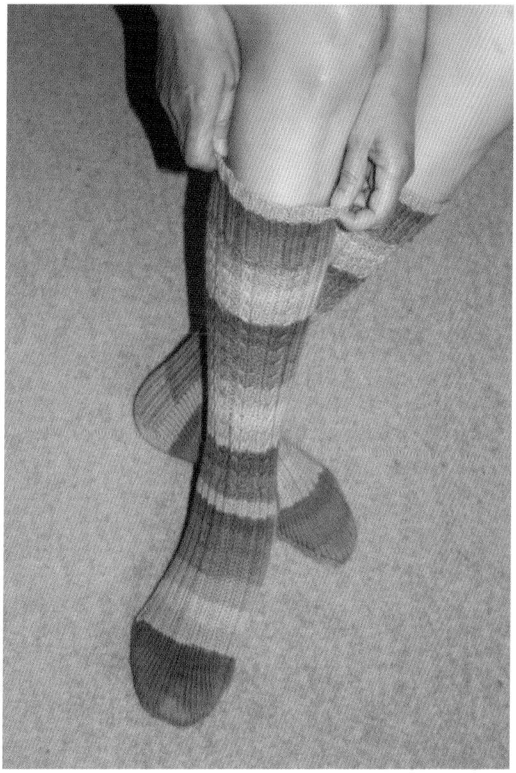

The Arctic Tern sock is ribbed to comfortably grip the leg.

For a cuff down sock

First of all, decide which type of pattern you want for the cuff – simple rib or something a little more complex – as this will affect whether you need an odd or even number of stitches, or a multiple of a specific number if the cuff is cabled or patterned.

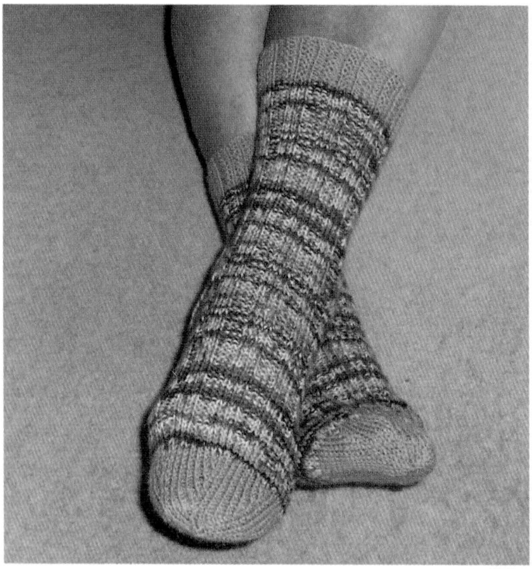

Longer socks like the Mallard are ideal for boots.

The instructions below are written as though the sock is being worked on a set of four double-pointed needles. But it is a simple matter to follow them using whichever type of needles you prefer.

Based on the measurements taken as described in Chapter 1, work out how many stitches you need to cast on for the cuff.

Example

With a tension of 28sts to 10cm/4in and a leg measurement of 25cm/10in you will need to cast on 70sts. For a 1×1 rib this will be perfect as it divides evenly by two, but for a 2×2 rib you would need to cast on 68 or 72 to divide exactly by four. Similarly, if you would like a cabled cuff of 2 stitches purled and 4 cabled, your stitches will need to be divisible by 6: so 66 or 72.

Note: these numbers are correct for socks knitted in the round but they will need added edge stitches for socks worked on two needles.

Remembering that all ribbing is more stretchy than stocking stitch, the lower number is probably best to stop the socks from falling down. However, so that the cast on edge is not too tight, use a needle one or two sizes larger for the first two rounds.

For a plain sock the number of cast-on stitches can now be continued for the leg. If you want a lace or cabled pattern you may need to change the number of stitches here to accommodate the repeat. Work to the required measurement then decide on the shape of the heel: a flap heel and gusset or one made from short rows. If you prefer to work short rows and your heel is fairly high work a few rows straight before starting the shaping. Whichever heel shape is chosen it is usually worked on half the number of stitches of the leg, leaving the rest on a spare needle. The change to this is where the sock has a pattern that needs to be centred over the instep. Then you need to decide which stitches to move, either to the heel or the instep, to make the most pleasing arrangement.

Heel with flap and gusset

Work back and forth on half the number of stitches, leaving those for the instep on two spare needles until the heel is completed. Working back and forth on two needles, slip the first stitch of every row until the heel is the required depth based on your measurements or for the same number of rows as there are stitches in the heel. Next the heel needs to be turned by working across a portion of the stitches decreasing at each turn. For a square heel shape, work two thirds of the stitches on the heel needle, decrease and work one stitch more. Turn and work the return row, across one third of the stitches, decrease and work one stitch more.

Example over 36sts

(That is a sock with 72 stitches in the rounds)

Row 1: sl1, k 23, ssk, k1 and turn.

Row 2: sl1, p12, p2tog, p1, turn.

Row 3: sl1, k12, ssk, k1, turn.

Rep the last 2 rows until all sts have been used ending on a purl row.

Sl1, k to end so that work is ready for picking up sts along the side of the heel.

Next, work the stitches to form the gusset. Pick up one stitch for each of the slipped stitches,

18 slipped stitches in the example above, make 1 (to avoid a potential hole) by knitting into the back of the horizontal bar between the heel stitches and the instep. Knit or work in pattern across the instep stitches, make 1 as before, then pick up the slipped stitches along the other side of the heel. Now work in rounds, decreasing one stitch on alternate rounds at the point where the heel meets the instep stitches. Decrease until the stitches are reduced to the number that were cast on or, if there were extra stitches required for the tension of a pattern, however many are needed for the foot. Continue on these stitches until the foot is the required length less approximately 2in for the toe.

Shape the toe using whichever method you prefer.

For a toe up sock

To work a flap and gusset heel on a toe up sock, work the gusset first by increasing the number of stitches in the foot to about twice the number in the sole. Turn the heel by working short rows and then knitting together one of the increased stitches with the last stitch of the heel flap until the stitches are back to the original number.

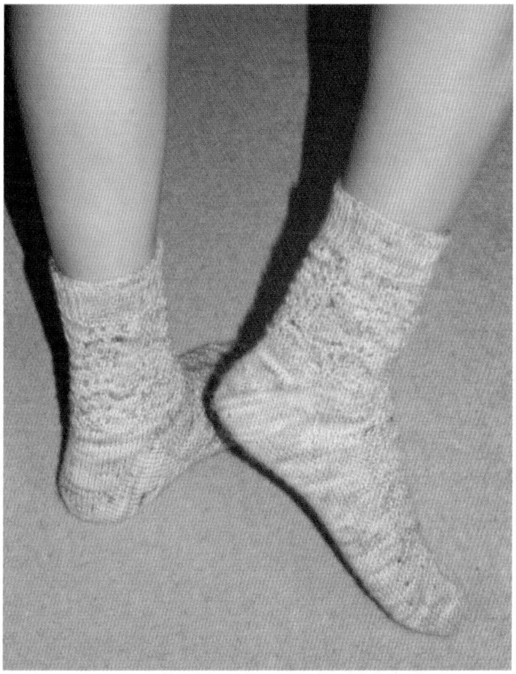

The Serin sock is knitted from the toe up.

Index